The Philadelphia Inquirer

WHAT A RUN!

Inside THE PHILADELPHIA EAGLES' Unforgettable 2024 Championship Season

SPECIAL COMMEMORATIVE BOOK

The Philadelphia Inquirer

Lisa Hughes, Publisher & CEO
Gabriel Escobar, Editor, Senior vice president
Charlotte Sutton, Managing editor
Patrick Kerkstra, Managing editor/content strategy
Michael Huang, Managing editor/Sports
Gary Potosky, Assistant managing editor/Sports
John Roberts and Jim Swan, book editors
Diamond Leung, Eagles editor
Gustav Elvin, DeAntae Prince, Isabella DiAmore, Kerith Gabriel, Maria McIlwain, contributing editors
Suzette Moyer, Design director
Danese Kenon, Managing editor/Visuals
Frank Wiese, Deputy director of video and photography
Jasmine Goldbland, Photo editor
Writers: EJ Smith, Olivia Reiner, Jeff McLane, Jeff Neiburg, Mike Sielski, Marcus Hayes, David Murphy, Alex Coffey
Inquirer staff photographers: Yong Kim, David Maialetti, Monica Herndon, Jose F. Moreno, Steven M. Falk

This book is available in quantity at special discounts for your group or organization.

For further information, contact:

Triumph Books LLC
814 North Franklin Street
Chicago, Illinois 60610
Phone: (312) 337-0747
www.triumphbooks.com

Printed in U.S.A.
ISBN: 978-1-63727-937-3

Content packaged by Mojo Media, Inc.
Joe Funk: Editor
Jason Hinman: Creative Director

Front cover photo by Yong Kim
Back cover photo by Monica Herndon

Contents

Introduction

By Jeff McLane

They arrived in the Deep South as slight underdogs, unlike two years ago in the desert when a group lacking in experience fell agonizingly short of glory. A fumble here, a pass interference penalty there — the Philadelphia Eagles' 38-35 loss in Super Bowl LVII was an outcome with many what-ifs.

But a rematch with the Kansas City Chiefs offered a chance at redemption and payback. And this time, a team that was as deep as the dedication of its fans denied Andy Reid and Patrick Mahomes a fourth title and a first-ever three-peat. Without an identifiable weakness, the Eagles walloped the top-heavy Chiefs in Super Bowl LIX, capping a season that seemed improbable a little over a year ago when a late-season implosion shook the franchise.

It might seem like a distant memory, but the collapse sowed the seeds for a rebirth. Nick Sirianni, nearly fired, rebuilt his coaching staff and brought back to Philly a wise old defensive sage in Vic Fangio. He gave up his offense and hired Kellen Moore. Architect Howie Roseman then executed an offseason plan to retool the roster by signing a running back who seemed to go against the general manager's philosophy but proved to be revelatory. Roseman also addressed holes on defense and found diamonds in free agency. And he drafted two cornerbacks who would perform well beyond their years.

Almost every new face delivered. Saquon Barkley, of course, would have the most impact. He dashed, juked, and reverse leaped into memory banks forever. He may have been denied an opportunity to eclipse a 40-year-old record, and he may have been snubbed the MVP award, but Barkley's season will be immortal. It will go down as one of the best in NFL history.

But the story of the 2024 Eagles can't be told without the contributions of other key additions. Linebacker Zack Baun entered under the radar, but he flourished after a position change. Safety C.J. Gardner-Johnson returned after a bitter divorce two years earlier and brought with him swagger and big hits. Mekhi Becton became another of offensive line coach Jeff Stoutland's reclamation projects with a successful switch from tackle to guard. Rookie corners Quinyon Mitchell and Cooper DeJean belied their age and played with confidence.

And then there were the mainstays and returnees. Veteran pillars like tackle Lane Johnson and defensive end Brandon Graham won second

The disappointment to close the 2023 season helped initiate the changes and laid the foundation for head coach Nick Sirianni and the Eagles to capture the second Vince Lombardi Trophy in franchise history. (David Maialetti / Staff Photographer)

titles, while cornerback Darius Slay finally got his. Receivers A.J. Brown and DeVonta Smith unselfishly accepted a bye-week alteration to a run-heavy offense, and thus, became champions. And the offensive line — with tackle Jordan Mailata, guard Landon Dickerson, center Cam Jurgens, Johnson and Becton — led the way on the ground and in protecting the franchise quarterback.

Jalen Hurts, mentioned last here but not in relation to his importance, may not have been as integral as he was in 2022, and certainly in going toe-to-toe with Mahomes two years ago. But the stoic 26-year-old answered the doubters, kept winning, and was voted Super Bowl MVP. That he would become the Eagles' first dual-threat quarterback to win a Super Bowl may surprise some who underestimated him from Houston to Tuscaloosa to Philly. But Hurts always embraced his mobility and to know him is to know he never doubted he would always "keep the main thing the main thing."

On defense, Jalen Carter was the linchpin. The second-year defensive tackle was a menace up front and just one of the Georgia Dawgs to leave an imprint on the season. Nolan Smith emerged as a force on the edge just as Graham went down with a triceps injury. Nakobe Dean paired with Baun at off-ball linebacker, and if not for a season-ending knee injury, would have been in between the lines at the Superdome. Defensive tackle Milton Williams, outside linebacker Josh Sweat, and safety Reed Blankenship were each catalysts at points whose contributions should not be forgotten.

Remember it all. The season-opening shootout win in Brazil. Barkley's drop vs. the Falcons. The disaster in Tampa. The bye-week look in the mirror and turnaround. Remember the spectacular like Smith's one-handed catch. The violent collisions from Gardner-Johnson and DeJean, who upended Derrick Henry. Remember the obstacles overcome. Hurts' injuries and struggles and absolution. Remember the playoffs. Barkley's 78-yard scoot in the snow. Carter's game-saving sack. The NFC championship confetti at Lincoln Financial Field.

And lastly, remember owner Jeffrey Lurie lifting his second Lombardi Trophy.

If the past is indeed prologue, then the seeds of the triumph in New Orleans were planted by their forefathers who wore the green and inflamed the civic spirit of millions, but also by what happened two years ago in Phoenix when the Eagles couldn't get past Reid, Mahomes, and the Chiefs. Eagles fans by and large predicted another title again, and maybe for the first time, their confidence was rewarded. The 2024 season was a tale in three acts, and it was a ride worth telling, but in the minds of those who experienced it and here on these pages, it will live forever. ■

Quarterback Jalen Hurts and wide receiver DeVonta Smith were in sync in Super Bowl LIX, connecting four times for 69 yards, including a 46-yard touchdown. (Yong Kim / Staff Photographer)

FEB. 9, 2025
NEW ORLEANS, LA.
EAGLES 40, CHIEFS 22

Call Them the Best

Eagles trounce the Chiefs to capture a second Super Bowl title

By Mike Sielski

There was no point, as the confetti feathered to the Superdome turf, as the Eagles and everyone who loves them let waves of euphoria wash over them Sunday night, to be anything but direct and succinct and true: What happened here was the greatest victory in the greatest season in the history of Philadelphia sports.

That is not an exaggeration, not an overstatement, not hyperbole. With their 40-22 victory in Super Bowl LIX over the Kansas City Chiefs, with a performance so dominant that only the caution and cynicism that once defined Philadelphia fandom could have caused doubt to seep into anyone's mind from the first quarter on, the Eagles completed a remarkable five months of football.

They played 21 games and won 18 of them. They did more than avenge their loss to the Chiefs two years ago in Super Bowl LVII. They did more than get the better of their old head coach, Andy Reid, and the best quarterback in the NFL, Patrick Mahomes. They did more than prevent the Chiefs from becoming the first team to win three consecutive Super Bowls. They made the Chiefs look foolish for even daring to think that a "three-peat" was possible. They made the league's reigning dynasty look like a bad high school team.

They did all this on the biggest stage in U.S. sports — no, U.S. culture. There is one night a year when one event serves as a shared experience for the country, and the Eagles owned that night.

This setting, these stakes, the popularity and reach and resonance of professional football in modern America — they are what separate the 2024-25 Eagles from the 1973-74 Flyers, from the 1982-83 76ers, from the 1980 or 2008 Phillies, even from the 2017-18 Eagles. From Nick Foles to the Philly Special, for winning the franchise's first Super Bowl, that team was a better story. This team is simply better. What's more, it was better in all the ways that aligned with the still-accurate clichés about its city, all the sensibilities that Philly people want in a football team.

The Eagles were the most productive rushing team in the NFL. They had Saquon Barkley — who even without having a spectacular Super Bowl, had a spectacular season, perhaps the best of any running back ever — and an offensive line that ground opponents into sand. They had, in Jalen Hurts, a

Rookie cornerback Cooper DeJean stunned Patrick Mahomes (15) and the Chiefs with a second-quarter pick-six to give the Eagles a commanding 17-0 lead. (Yong Kim / Staff Photographer)

quarterback who in this postseason erased any reservations about whether the Eagles could count on him to excel when the games mattered most. All he did Sunday night was run for 72 yards and a touchdown, throw for 221 yards and two more scores, and outplay Mahomes from start to finish.

They had, in Nick Sirianni, a head coach who wears his heart on his sleeve, on his shirt collar, on his pants, and on his socks. His players love him for it. They respect him for always being himself. Sirianni does what a 21st-century coach has to do, first and foremost, to succeed: He connects. It took him a while to get out of his own way in that regard, to not allow his emotions and insecurities to overwhelm him in the moment, but the results demonstrate that he has learned that valuable lesson.

And finally, the Eagles had the league's best defense — a defense directed by a wise old owl in Vic Fangio, a defense so good Sunday night that it sacked Mahomes six times, held him and the Chiefs to 23 total yards and one first down in the first half, forced him to fumble once, and intercepted him twice.

The first of those interceptions was the capstone to a sequence that changed everything about the direction and expectations of this game. The Eagles led by 10 points with 8 minutes, 38 seconds left in the second quarter. It was not a comfortable lead, not at that time, because a 10-point deficit has been nothing to Mahomes throughout his career. Hell, the Eagles had led Super Bowl LVII by 10 at halftime, and Mahomes, Reid, and the Chiefs spent that second half making Jonathan Gannon's head spin.

Not this time. On first down, Mahomes dropped back, and Josh Sweat sacked him. On second down, Mahomes dropped back, and Jalyx Hunt sacked him. On third down, Mahomes rolled right and fired

Wide receiver A.J. Brown had only three catches for 43 yards but made them count with a second-quarter touchdown to give the Eagles a 24-0 head start. (David Maialetti / Staff Photographer)

a pass toward the middle of the field — a no-no for any other quarterback, par for the course for him ... usually. Except Cooper DeJean picked it off and surged forward, and as he weaved through the Chiefs for a 38-yard touchdown, the sound within the Superdome kept rising, a crescendo that reaffirmed what had been clear all week here: New Orleans was overflowing with Eagles fans, and now they knew what was coming.

Their team shared that confidence. All week here, in every media availability, in every public interaction, the Eagles' coaches and players projected a sense of relaxed self-assurance. It was a striking thing to witness, in part because it was so obvious and so widespread. There was no excessive exuberance from DeJean, from Quinyon Mitchell, from Hunt, from the youngest players on the roster, from the guys who had never been here before. From the veterans, there was nothing but a radiating feeling of calm, as if the outcome were certain all along. *We know we are better than the Chiefs. We are supposed to be here, and we are supposed to win.*

"It comes down to the character of the guys you have," tackle Lane Johnson said. "Do you have guys who care about money, or do you have guys who really love football?"

The Eagles answered that question Sunday night, and no Philadelphia team has ever met a comparable challenge with such poise and pure force. This was no upset. This was no Cinderella story. This was no surprise to anyone who watched the 2024-25 Eagles. Call them what they are. Call them the best. ■

Linebacker Zack Baun celebrates picking off yet another pass from Patrick Mahomes, one of two key early takeaways for the Eagles defense. (Yong Kim / Staff Photographer)

Built for More

Nick Sirianni is at the doorstep of an Eagles dynasty with Jalen Hurts and a dominant young defense

By Marcus Hayes

When all the confetti had fallen and the crowd had all gone home, Nick Sirianni sat on a blue TV crate and hung his weary head. He couldn't find his family. He couldn't believe his fate.

He had no phone. No bodyguard. It was just him, alone, quiet, with his thoughts.

A year before, he'd had to convince Jeffrey Lurie that he was still the right man to lead the Eagles.

On Sunday night, Sirianni led them to the second Super Bowl championship in franchise history.

He blew out Andy Reid and the Kansas City Chiefs, 40-22, in Super Bowl LIX, the same coach and the same team that beat Sirianni two years ago. Sirianni knows, with a 26-year-old quarterback as Super Bowl MVP, a young defense, a peerless GM, and a generous owner, there is no good reason he shouldn't be coaching in this game again and again and again.

"Oh, yeah," said Lurie as he prowled the Superdome field.

"Why not?" said third-year defensive tackle Jordan Davis, a cornerstone of the best D in the league. "I mean, now we know what it takes."

It takes talent, and this is the most-talented group the franchise has ever had, and they're mostly young, unlike the 2017 team that promised more than it could deliver. On the Art Museum steps on a frigid February afternoon, Doug Pederson vowed to 1 million freezing, faithful Eagles fans that this sort of celebration would be "the new norm."

He was right. He was just seven years premature. And, even though he won Super Bowl LII, it turned out that Pederson was the wrong coach. And it turned out that Nick Sirianni was the right coach. Improbably. Incredibly.

That's right. That guy.

The guy who channeled Barney Fife in his historically awful introductory news conference in 2021. The guy who talked about Flower Power his first season, then had flowers thrown at him from the stands after a loss. The guy who taunted Eagles

Josh Sweat (19) and Jalyx Hunt (58) take down Patrick Mahomes in the second quarter. The Eagles sacked Mahomes six times in the win. (David Maialetti / Staff Photographer)

fans at home after Game 5 this season, then had to apologize for his arrogance.

That guy.

That guy's a Super Bowl champion. That guy, whose deal expires this time next year, is going to get a contract extension worth as much as $20 million per season.

Lurie refused Sunday to discuss Sirianni's future, but he gushed about his past and present.

"Nick epitomizes our culture — the resilience, the genuineness," Lurie said.

Nobody else even interviewed Sirianni in 2021, and he's made a slew of mistakes in his four seasons, but he stands atop the sporting world now. Does Lurie feel validated? Does he think Sirianni feels validated?

"Yes," Lurie said, "and yes."

Nick?

He'd hugged about 100 people and taken 17 pictures (one with Freddie Mitchell and Brian Westbrook) and done 11 official interviews and signed two autographs and was striding toward the tunnel to leave the field.

"Ah, I don't really think that way," he said.

Really?

Eagles fans pressed against the railing and celebrated him. He tipped his new Super Bowl champion hat to the crowd, then took it off and tossed it to a kid. Then a guy yelled out:

"Never a doubt!"

Sirianni looked back at me, smirked, and rolled his eyes.

"Yeah," he said, "'Never a doubt.'"

No one has never not doubted Sirianni in Philly. They'll never doubt him again.

They lost to the Chiefs by a field goal two years ago, but they won Sunday night by six field goals. They led by 24 at halftime. They looked utterly unbeatable against the best AFC team in the past decade.

Maybe they are unbeatable. They've won 16 of 17 games, including the most important one. Maybe they're the NFC's version of the Chiefs, who have been in five of the last six Super Bowls. Maybe this time it really is the "New Norm" for the Eagles.

As Davis said, why not? Why not three or four more Super Bowls this decade? Top to bottom, they're built for it. Credit GM Howie Roseman some, or even credit Lurie, but neither one of them is in the locker room nor on the sideline. Sirianni is. They buy the groceries. He makes the meal.

The ingredients are fresh.

Quarterback Jalen Hurts is 26 and under contract for four more seasons. The league's best running back, Saquon Barkley, is signed for two more years; on Sunday, he broke the single-season rushing record (playoffs included). There's no real reason he can't do it twice more. Why? Because three of the five offensive linemen are under contract for at least two more seasons, and because A.J. Brown and DeVonta Smith, the league's best receiver tandem, can be Birds together through 2028. They each had a touchdown catch in Super Bowl LIX.

Offensive coordinator Kellen Moore is expected to stay in New Orleans and become the Saints head coach, but defensive coordinator Vic Fangio, now 66, doesn't want to be a head coach again. God bless him.

Sunday night was a Vic Fangio fever dream.

The defense surrendered zero points until 34 seconds remained in the third quarter. Zero. There was a pick-six, and another interception set up Hurts' touchdown pass to Brown. Second-year defensive tackle Jalen Carter, the team's best defender, pressured Patrick Mahomes and forced a punt on the first possession, setting a tone. Davis had a sack. Rookie end Jalyx Hunt had a half-sack. Second-year edge rusher Nolan Smith pressured Mahomes and forced a punt on the Chiefs' second possession. Rookie cornerback Cooper DeJean intercepted a pass and ran it back 38 yards for a touchdown in the second quarter. Second-year defensive tackle Moro Ojomo dropped Isiah Pacheco for a 2-yard loss. Rookie corner Quinyon Mitchell was too good for Mahomes to challenge.

The future is bright. Even kicker Jake Elliott has four more years left on his deal. He'd been inconsistent this season, but he made all eight kicks Sunday night. Flawless.

OK, the Eagles weren't exactly flawless. It just felt that way.

On third-and-10 from the Chiefs' 30 late in the first quarter, facing pressure from a blitz, Hurts floated a duck toward the right pylon, where Brown was covered by one player and it was intercepted. It was an aberration. Hurts hadn't thrown an interception in nine games.

By halftime, the only player in midnight green who hadn't mattered much was Barkley, the player who'd mattered most all season. The Chiefs forced Hurts to beat them. Barkley had 18 yards on his first nine rushes and finished with just 57 yards on 25 carries.

Hurts obliged the Chiefs. He was 17 for 22 with 221 yards and two touchdowns, with completions of 15, 20, 22, 22, 27, and 46 yards, the last one a touchdown to Smith that made it 34-0 late in the third quarter. He added 72 rushing yards on 11 runs, breaking his own Super Bowl record of 70 rushing yards by a quarterback, and he scored on a Tush Push to boot.

Easiest MVP vote in years ... because Sirianni wasn't eligible. All he gets is a ring. He deserves it.

It's been four long years, and it took a while for Sirianni to find his feet. If nothing else, he's adept at self-examination and self-deprecation.

"The genuineness can create emotional ups and downs. That's human," Lurie explained. "I think everyone relates to that. Yet his attention to detail and his depth of thought ... sometimes people miss that leadership."

After just seven games as a head coach in 2021, Sirianni surrendered play-calling to former OC Shane Steichen but remained the offense's architect. After Steichen left for the Indianapolis head coaching job, Sirianni took a larger role with new OC Brian Johnson, whom he fired after last season. Moore signed on under the condition that Sirianni recuse himself from almost all offensive responsibilities.

It worked.

Sirianni left the defense to Fangio. He oversaw Moore's game plans and play-calling but added little. But then, that's what most of the best head coaches in history have done. They delegated.

But Sirianni played a crucial role in turning Hurts' season around. From the start of the 2023 season through Game 4 of 2024, Hurts led the NFL in turnovers. Sirianni put Hurts in a "straitjacket" — Hurts' word — leaned on Barkley, and trusted the defense. Hurts has turned the ball over four times in his 15 games since.

In games he's both started and finished, the team is 14-0.

Credit that crazy coach. ∎

Years in the Making

Jalen Hurts named Super Bowl MVP after leading domination of Chiefs

By EJ Smith

Jalen Hurts emerged from the Eagles locker room with his song of choice blaring loudly enough to reach him and his trophy in an adjacent hallway.

Cigar in mouth, Lombardi in hand, the Eagles quarterback leaned onto the wall, slid down to the floor and let the moment wash over him. He shook his head in disbelief in between the lines of "Happy Feelin's" by Frankie Beverly and Maze, singing along to the song by his favorite artist as it reverberated into the walls of the Caesars Superdome after the Eagles' 40-22 win over the Kansas City Chiefs in Super Bowl LIX.

I've seen the light, I watched it shine down on me...

Two years after arguably the best performance of his career came in a Super Bowl loss to the Chiefs, Hurts had answered the call for the Eagles in a blowout win that vaults him into rarified air. The kid who led a plucky high school team in Channelview, Texas, the kid who got benched in the national championship game as a sophomore at Alabama, and the man leading the Eagles back to the biggest stage two years after watching the red-and-yellow confetti fall on him and his teammates. A champion at last.

I'm gonna spread my wings, yeah, I'm gonna tell all I see...

Hurts, if nothing else, is intentional. From the cigar the 26-year-old plucked out of a leather pouch to the Jordan Brand goggles with the word "CHAMP" inscribed on the lenses, to the song choice that accompanied the lasting image of Hurts' transformative night, it was clear this plan was years in the making.

So little of his football career has gone according to those plans. A public benching at Alabama led to him transferring to Oklahoma and getting drafted to a team that, at the time, thought it had an entrenched franchise quarterback in Carson Wentz. Even after an MVP-caliber 2022 season ended in a Super Bowl loss, questions lingered about Hurts' ability to truly join the ranks of elite quarterbacks.

Reflecting on the plan and the deviations from it in his postgame news conference, Hurts seemingly fought back tears processing the improbable path he took to leading the Eagles to their second Super Bowl title in franchise history.

"It's not normal," Hurts said. "It's been a very unprecedented journey, and the journey is — it's always the beginning until it's the end. I think — it means a lot. Quantifying all that work over the years, embracing everything, taking every challenge head on and taking every joy and moment

Eagles quarterback Jalen Hurts and coach Nick Sirianni celebrate after the win over the Chiefs in New Orleans. (Yong Kim / Staff Photographer)

of achievement and success head on as well. I'm processing them all as one."

Unbeknownst to him, his father had a similar sentiment an hour before, waiting for the final whistle before celebrating with his son as green, white, and black confetti descended upon the field and the Eagles fight song filled the surrounding tunnels. It should come as no surprise; the similarities between the two stretch beyond the resemblance they share into the way they think and the way they present those thoughts as well.

The two were playing pool in the basement of Hurts' home after the NFC championship game, Averion Hurts Sr. told The Inquirer, when he reminded his son how uncommon his latest accomplishment was.

"My response was, 'Two Super Bowls in three years is not normal,'" Averion Sr. said. "This ain't some normal [stuff.] We just laughed and kept it moving, but for me, I'm just so happy for him. I understand what it means to him, I understand how hard he works. I understand how he is as a person, and it ain't always easy to deal with, but I understand what this means to him."

"You know, F.A.F.O?" Averion Sr. said, alluding to the sentiment *mess around and find out*. "We found out tonight."

Hurts' performance will certainly silence most doubters. He finished 17-for-22 for 221 yards, two touchdowns and one interception, adding another 72 rushing yards along with one rushing touchdown on a quarterback sneak. His rushing total set a new mark for a quarterback in Super Bowl history, breaking his own record from two years ago by 2 yards.

Hurts also became the fourth Black quarterback to win a Super Bowl, joining Doug Williams, Russell Wilson, and Patrick Mahomes. There's a case to be made he is the first true dual-threat quarterback to win a championship as well, although his brightest moments came operating out of the pocket Sunday with timely throws to A.J. Brown and DeVonta Smith to pad the Eagles' lead.

"Jalen's special and the criticism just blows my mind because I think he's so special," Eagles coach Nick Sirianni said. "And he's won so many games and works his butt off. He just continues to get better and can block out everything, focus on the task at hand of getting better and put himself in the position to win each week. He does a great job of that and he had an unbelievable game today when we needed him to."

Standing outside the pulsing locker room party, Eagles owner Jeffrey Lurie added, "Going into this game, it was the least of my worries. I knew he would play great, just as he did two years ago. You worry about almost everything, that's one thing I didn't even think about, I just said, 'We've got the quarterback.' He's 26, incredibly clutch, he knows what correlates with winning."

Midway through Lurie's answer, the music cut and restarted with Hurts' preferred song. The proverbial quarterback had his moment, and gave the Eagles reason to believe he could deliver more just like it in the future.

Happy feelin's in the air... ■

Jalen Hurts was a force on the ground in Super Bowl LIX, totaling 72 rushing yards. (David Maialetti / Staff Photographer)

ROAD TO
THE TITLE

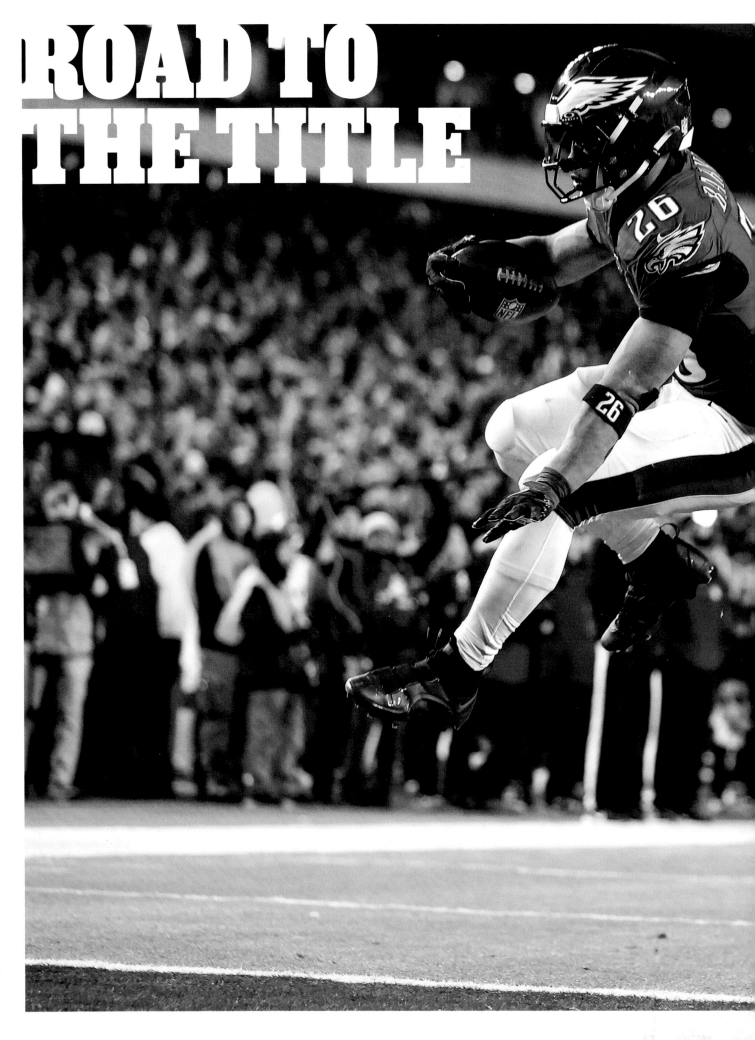

SEPT. 6, 2024
SÃO PAULO, BRAZIL
EAGLES 34, PACKERS 29

The World at His Feet

Saquon Barkley saves the Eagles in Brazilian misadventure

By David Murphy

They needed a star. Desperately. Nobody needed one more than the commish. A savior. That's what Roger Goodell needed. It's exactly what he got.

He, and the Eagles, riding in the wake of two massive quads.

Friday night at Corinthians Arena was supposed to be a lot of things: an international showcase for the NFL, a coming-out party for a revamped Eagles defense, a hotly contested marquee game with serious playoff implications.

It started out as a circus.

Then, Saquon Barkley stole the show. He did so mercifully, snatching victory from the jaws of defeat. In a literal sense for the Eagles as far as the win is concerned, in a figurative sense for the NFL.

Three touchdowns, 132 all-purpose yards, 109 of them on the ground. A bell cow performance, inside zones, outside zones, wheel routes, interrupted by the occasional outburst of emotion, a flex and a scream and a nod of the helmet at his latest imposition of force and will.

Barkley is a Man, a Man with a capital M, a Man unlike any the Eagles have had at running back since Wilbert Montgomery. That's a funny thing to say here in 2024. The Eagles have spent much of the last decade leading the league-wide depression that has gripped the running back profession. They traded away LeSean McCoy, won a Super Bowl with Jay Ajayi and LeGarrette Blount, bid adieu to Miles Sanders, replaced him on the cheap with D'Andre Swift. The first rule of Howie Club is you don't talk about Howie Club and the second rule is you don't spend big money on a running back.

Thing is, Barkley isn't just a running back. He is an exception who proves the rule.

You saw it throughout the Eagles' 34-29 win over the Packers here in the NFL's first regular-season game in Brazil (not to mention its first international season opener). Barkley is just built differently, inside and out. The first of his three touchdowns showcased his top-level receiving ability. Not only did he get a couple of steps on a couple of defenders on a wheel route down the left sideline, but he also managed to keep his feet in bounds while coming down with the catch.

He spent the rest of the night reminding us that he can still ground and pound. His 11-yard

Jalen Hurts hands off the ball to Saquon Barkley during the Eagles' season opener at Corinthians Arena in São Paulo, Brazil. (Jose F. Moreno / Staff Photographer)

touchdown run late in the second quarter was a testament to the force that he brings once he reaches top speed. Five yards down the field, you realized he wasn't going to be stopped.

Twenty-four carries for 109 yards. Sounds almost nostalgic, doesn't it? The Eagles weren't supposed to believe in that kind of thing anymore. But it sure is nice that they had it.

Barkley was a stabilizing force on a night when the defense looked disconcertingly inept under first-year coordinator Vic Fangio. Heralded free agent signee Bryce Huff was nowhere to be found. The box score says he played. But somebody else will have to confirm it. On the rare occasion the Packers were stopped, it mostly was self-inflicted.

Meanwhile, the current quarterback had some moments that looked an awful lot like the ones that came to define the last guy. Three turnovers, including two awful interceptions. Jalen Hurts had some decent moments, some excellent throws. But there was plenty of head-scratching to do.

As for the game itself and the Brazilian experiment, there were several moments early on when it flirted with debacle. It took the Packers two hours to make the 20-mile trip from their hotel to the stadium, thanks to this city's infamous rush hour traffic. The field appeared to have all of the traction of a 100-yard banana peel. Late in the first quarter, the Eagles and Packers had combined for more penalty yards than yards of total offense.

In the end, Barkley was the headline. The Eagles were the victors. They need to be better. Much better. They'll at least get to do it at 1-0. ■

Saquon Barkley scored three touchdowns in his Eagles debut, logging 24 carries for 109 yards against the Packers. (David Maialetti / Staff Photographer)

'A Superstar, Mega-Athlete'

Zack Baun is still growing as an NFL linebacker

By Olivia Reiner | Sept. 15, 2024

A casual viewing of an open-gym basketball game at the Brown Deer High School field house in the summer of 2014 quickly turned into a recruiting trip for Rob Green.

The head coach of the school's football team in the northern suburbs of Milwaukee, Green had just departed a weightlifting and conditioning session when he came across the game and began to chat with spectators. A mystery student-athlete on the court who elevated "like he was on a pogo stick," Green said, pulled off a one-handed dunk and interrupted Green's conversation.

Green did a double take. The football coach didn't recognize the player. The school's basketball coach enlightened an inquisitive Green.

That's Zack Baun. He moved into the district.

That, in Green's mind, was a future member of the Brown Deer football team if he had a say in the matter.

Baun was a standout basketball player in Wisconsin who had grown disinterested in football. West Bend East, his former high school where he was a wide receiver, lacked a strong program. But at the behest of a friend, the incoming junior decided to give the sport another chance and accepted Green's invitation to a July football camp.

He wouldn't remain a receiver for long. After snaring a pass on a slant route, getting vertical, and

scoring a touchdown on a 40-yard play, Baun threw the ball back to the heir apparent at quarterback for 50. Heir apparent? Apparently not.

During training camp, Green offered Baun the chance to start at quarterback. The 17-year-old responded with an affirmative refrain that he would repeat several times throughout his football career when faced with a position change: "If it's going to help the team."

"That's been a common trend throughout my career," said Baun, who went on to account for 94 touchdowns passing and rushing through 22 games in his two-year Brown Deer career. "From that time, I guess I've always just been an athlete. I can do a lot of different things and whatever I try to do, or whatever I set out to do, I want to be the best at it."

Ten years and two more position changes later, the versatile Baun is settling in as a starting inside linebacker with the Eagles alongside Nakobe Dean, breaking out with a two-sack, 15-tackle performance in Week 1 against the Green Bay Packers. He began to learn the position with the New Orleans Saints, the team that drafted him in the third round out of Wisconsin in 2020.

But the 27-year-old Baun has mostly served as a core special-teamer throughout his five-year NFL career, until now. Each challenge has prepared him

Linebacker Zack Baun sacks Panthers quarterback Bryce Young during the Eagles' Week 14 win.
(Monica Herndon / Staff Photographer)

for the next one, leading to his first full-time starting gig in the NFL.

'A superstar, mega-athlete'

When Paul Chryst would recruit high schoolers for his Wisconsin football program as its head coach from 2015-22, some of them were close-minded about the positions they would play at the Division I level. Baun wasn't, he recalled.

At 6-foot-3, 221 pounds as an incoming freshman in 2015, Baun was recruited as a gray-shirt linebacker by the previous coaching staff under Gary Andersen. The new regime wanted to keep Baun, a local product, and transition him to a weak side outside linebacker in its 3-4 base defense. The coaches admired his athleticism — Tim Tibesar, the former Wisconsin outside linebackers coach, saw the football and basketball highlights — and thought he had the right frame for the role.

"Whatever we thought was best for him, he'd have gone all-in on it," said Chryst, who made Baun a full member of the 2015 class upon his hiring.

As a redshirt in his first year at Wisconsin, Baun learned the position behind the likes of Joe Schobert, Vince Biegel, and T.J. Watt, who each went on to an NFL career. According to Andrew Van Ginkel, the current Minnesota Vikings linebacker who transferred to Wisconsin in 2017, linebackers in the Badgers program possessed a similar makeup. They weren't heavily recruited, five-star prospects. The chips on their shoulders spurred a strong work ethic.

Each player also boasted a versatile skill set. According to Tibesar, Wisconsin looked for a "different guy" to play outside linebacker compared to other programs.

"We wanted these edges to be true linebackers, rather than just defensive ends with their hand down," Tibesar said. "And we asked them to be able to drop into coverage and do coverage things in addition to being rushers."

Baun cultivated those skills and that work ethic in practice before putting it all together at Camp Randall Stadium. Cole Van Lanen, the former Wisconsin offensive tackle who now plays for the Jacksonville Jaguars, remembered "that tenacity and that quickness" that Baun boasted in one-on-one pass rush reps. He excelled at slapping tackles' hands down on his speed rush, according to Logan Bruss, another ex-Wisconsin tackle who now plays for the Los Angeles Rams.

Game action on defense wasn't easy for Baun to come by at first. He missed the entire 2017 season with a foot injury. Patience, persistence, and a positive attitude paid off. Baun started all 27 games in his final two seasons in 2018 and 2019, ranking second in the Big Ten in his final year with 19½ tackles for losses and 12½ sacks. He also notched six pass breakups and two interceptions through the two seasons.

"He had a real knack for bending the corner, being an athlete, playing in space, which I know was helpful in that scheme, because he can then drop out and cover some slot receivers or even a running back, depending on where he was on the field," said Jared Thomas, a former Northwestern offensive lineman who played against Baun. "Zack was always a superstar, mega-athlete."

Preparing for an opportunity

Baun bulked up to 238 pounds by the time he reached his draft year in 2020, but he was still undersized compared to most NFL edge rushers. He was more likely to land a job as an off-the-ball linebacker at the next level, a projection that Bobby King, the Eagles inside linebackers coach, agreed with while scouting Baun in the same role with the Houston Texans.

"I saw it just in the limited reps at Wisconsin," King said. "I thought he really, really could get off blocks well and I just thought I saw a really, really good ceiling coming out of college."

Like he did at Wisconsin, Baun learned from talented veterans in New Orleans, including Demario Davis and Kwon Alexander, who have three Pro Bowls and one All-Pro nod between them. He also welcomed insight from Pete Werner, whom the Saints drafted in the second round in 2021 out of Ohio State and had played the position longer than Baun had.

Baun never earned a full-time starting opportunity in Dennis Allen's 4-3 defensive scheme. He took the same approach to adversity as he did at Wisconsin, maintaining his patience, persistence, and positive attitude throughout four seasons with the Saints.

"If you're not playing, if you're in a backup position, if you're on special teams, it's important to keep learning and keep growing, 'cause you never know when your opportunity is going to come," Baun said.

In 2023, he started to see the field more often. Baun lined up on the edge and in the box while executing a variety of assignments in both alignments, from rushing the passer to stopping the run to dropping into coverage. The snaps in the box were more of a rarity (33 compared to 252 on the edge, according to Pro Football Focus), but he flashed enough instincts off the ball to pique the interest of Vic Fangio.

The Eagles' defensive coordinator had previous success finding a role for another versatile Wisconsin linebacker during his one-year stint with the Miami Dolphins in 2023. At the outset of

the season, the Dolphins had two talented edge rushers in Bradley Chubb and Jaelan Phillips, so Fangio approached the fifth-year veteran Van Ginkel about taking more snaps from the inside linebacker position to get on the field.

Van Ginkel said he saw the vision: He was a good athlete in space who could cover and blitz from the box, which would increase the likelihood of a mismatch in pass protection against a running back. He thrived under Fangio, going from 29% of the defensive snaps in 2022 to 66% in 2023 and finishing the season with career highs in sacks (six) and pass breakups (eight).

While Van Ginkel was still more of an on-the-ball linebacker in Fangio's system, both players are versatile in their defensive abilities. Van Ginkel said his experience exploiting different matchups last season can work in Baun's favor, too, and in a single showing against the Packers, it already did.

"I'm just proud of him, 'cause he didn't get [many] opportunities in New Orleans," said Van Ginkel, who signed a two-year, $20 million deal with the Vikings after his standout season. "But to see him go to Philadelphia and get that opportunity, get the chance to show what he's capable of and play at a high level, obviously I always knew that he could do what he did against Green Bay. He's a heck of a player and a heck of an athlete."

Room to grow

Going into Week 1, Baun said he wanted to play freely. As a result, the motor and toughness that Nick Sirianni raved about during training camp showed up on the field. The head coach highlighted a play in which Baun came off the edge on a bubble screen and quickly dropped 5 yards into coverage, tackling Emmanuel Wilson for no gain.

In a short window, King has learned that Baun is his own harshest critic, even after the best defensive performance of his NFL career. The coach preaches the "24-hour rule" in his room, giving his players a day to move on from a game, good or bad.

"He's still a baby at this position," King said. "He's making plays and stuff, but if you ask him if he left some plays out there, there's still a huge step to take with his game."

Still, Baun set a foundation for how he can leverage his versatility in Fangio's defense and help the group find collective success. Thomas, now a center for the USFL's Memphis Showboats, said that offensive lines typically account for a middle or weakside linebacker in pass protection on base downs. But in pressure situations, he said that a player like Baun who can blitz from the box can put an "offensive line in peril" if it has to account for him in protection, potentially leaving a free rusher on the edge.

Of course, Baun is also familiar with rushing the passer from the edge, as he did at Wisconsin.

"The fact that he can fly around, be an athlete, which I think plays to his strengths, but that he understands blitzing from a linebacker position, getting lined up on the edge," Thomas said. "It's like he's right back in Madison, and that's going to be such a plus for [the Eagles] defense."

Baun also possesses an ability to disguise the coverage before the snap and throw off an offense. A simulated pressure in which Baun showed blitz off the edge, then dropped into coverage in the third quarter, forced Jordan Love to make a bad decision by attempting to target Luke Musgrave over the middle of the field. Baun's coverage underneath the route allowed Reed Blankenship to swoop in and snare an interception.

"Anything you can do to keep offensive coordinators there late at night — 'cause we're there late at night — an extra hour or two always makes you feel kind of good, so they have to game plan for him," King explained.

This season, Baun will attempt to pull off the objective of the one-year, "prove-it" deal he signed with the Eagles in the offseason. The intrinsic motivation to be the best athlete he can be has intensified while making yet another kind of transition in his life. Baun is a first-time father to his son, Elian, who was born in April. He said that his whole world, including his perspective on his football career, changed when he became a father.

"People tell you about that, but you don't know it until you really feel it yourself," Baun said. "But just providing is my ultimate gift to him and my family. And that's always the goal, to sign a multiyear deal, right?

"You just want to make the most out of this short opportunity that we have in the league."

Sixteen more regular-season games, at least 16 more opportunities for Baun to seize as an impact player in the Eagles defense. ■

Zack Baun developed into one of the NFL's elite defenders in 2024, earning All-Pro honors in the process. (Yong Kim / Staff Photographer)

SEPT. 16, 2024
LINCOLN FINANCIAL FIELD
FALCONS 22, EAGLES 21

'Take the Lick and Move On'

The Eagles falter as Kirk Cousins and the Falcons get the last laugh

By Jeff Neiburg

Jalen Hurts leaned in close as Saquon Barkley sat at his locker stall and, with a hoarse voice, the Eagles quarterback told Barkley that he trusts him every time with the game on the line. Hurts extended a fist, Barkley gave it a bump with his own, and the running back then started to get dressed.

There's an uncomfortable thing that happens in professional football locker rooms. Some reporters and camera operators watched that interaction and then, inch by inch, as Barkley clothed himself, they moved closer to his stall. Barkley knew what was coming. He's new to the Eagles but not new to a big media market.

You need both hands to count the number of reasons the Eagles lost to Atlanta on Monday night, maybe even a few toes, but if you isolate one play that flipped the whole thing, it was Barkley dropping a third-and-3 throw from Hurts with the Eagles ahead by three, the clock inside the two-minute warning, and the Falcons out of timeouts.

"I make that catch, game's over," Barkley said.

Instead, the incomplete pass forced a fourth down, stopped the clock, caused the Eagles to kick a field goal, and opened the door for an improbable game-winning drive by Kirk Cousins, who torched the Eagles' secondary, going 70 yards on six plays in 1 minute, 5 seconds to silence the Lincoln Financial Field crowd.

"I dropped the ball," Barkley said. "I let my team down today. Shouldn't have put the defense in that position."

There will be quibbling over the play call for days. Why didn't the Eagles run the ball, take more time off the clock if they didn't convert, and kick a field goal if needed, giving Cousins and the Falcons offense less time to score? There are still unanswered questions, too, about the sequence that led to the drop. Prior to the play, the Eagles put a heavy package onto the field with an extra tackle, Fred Johnson, and called a timeout before the play clock expired. It's unclear what the plan was, but Eagles coach Nick Sirianni said it did involve taking that timeout. But the ensuing package didn't feature Johnson.

"They were running a certain defense and junking it up in the middle, so we were trying to go around the outside and it didn't work," Sirianni said.

It is probably being too results-oriented to just blame the play call. Barkley was wide open, and Hurts put the ball right on his hands. There were elements of risk involved in the call, sure, but the Eagles got their best offensive player — with A.J. Brown out of action — open and threw a high-percentage pass in his direction.

Barkley said he wasn't surprised by the decision to throw. It is a play the Eagles have had plenty of

Though Saquon Barkley claimed responsibility for the Eagles' loss after a pivotal dropped ball on third down, the team's ineffective defensive line and passing offense also contributed to the result. (Yong Kim / Staff Photographer)

reps running, he and Hurts both said.

"Once I knew it, I thought it was a great play call," he said. "I just got to make the catch."

Had the Eagles won, it would have been largely because of Barkley and Hurts, who combined for 180 rushing yards. Instead, in a cruel twist, it was Barkley's drop and Hurts' poor decision on the final drive, after the Falcons took the lead, to throw an ill-advised deep ball into the hands of a waiting Jessie Bates.

Barkley, through two games, has been as good as advertised. He has rushed for 204 yards and has three total touchdowns. He has added another 44 receiving yards with six catches on seven targets. It's that final stat, though, that has the Eagles at 1-1 instead of 2-0.

"We just didn't make the play in that moment, and I trust him in every moment," Hurts said. "He's a hell of a player. He gave us a big spark in those moments, and it just wasn't for us tonight."

Said safety C.J. Gardner-Johnson: "It's football,

bro. [Stuff] happens. You can't fault a guy for making one mistake. It's other things that led to a loss, but you can't fault one guy and put one thing on somebody's shoulders for a whole game."

It was, however, one of the easiest places to point, and Barkley wasn't looking to point anywhere else.

"I could sit here and complain and be upset about it or I could be a professional athlete and go back to the drawing board and take the lick and move on and get better from it," Barkley said. "I've made that play multiple times. I've missed that play before, too. I just got to be better. I let my team down. I got to man up to it, I got to own it, which I'm doing. I could promise those guys in this locker room that I'm going to be better from it.

"It definitely sucks. Any loss sucks. But the game comes down to a few plays and it hurts a little more when you're the one who's making a mistake on that play." ∎

SEPT. 22, 2024
NEW ORLEANS, LA.
EAGLES 15, SAINTS 12

Next Man Up

Dallas Goedert sparks a winning drive against the Saints

By EJ Smith

At the behest of A.J. Brown, Dallas Goedert put the cape on for the Eagles on Sunday afternoon.

The Eagles tight end was the lone member of the offense's primary trio of receiving options left for the closing moments of the team's too-close-for-comfort game against the Saints. With Brown sidelined with a hamstring injury and DeVonta Smith leaving early with a concussion, it was time for Goedert to play superhero on his own.

He did just that, delivering a 61-yard catch-and-run to set up the go-ahead touchdown in the Eagles' 15-12 win over the Saints at the Caesars Superdome.

"I never want to let my team down," Goedert said. "We get the ball with two minutes left and we need a touchdown, that's situational ball that we work on all the time. We were able to get it done today."

Goedert came into Sunday with seven catches for 69 yards over two games with a surprisingly limited role in the offense. That changed against the Saints, with Goedert receiving a team-high 11 targets and catching 10 of them for a career-high 170 yards.

"We called his number quite a bit today," Eagles quarterback Jalen Hurts said. "And he showed up. A lot of guys showed up. He had a great moment, I'm proud of him."

His most pivotal target came with the Eagles facing an uphill battle on third-and-16 with the game hanging in the balance. Hurts changed plays at the line of scrimmage after a pre-snap motion by Saquon Barkley tipped off that the Saints were in man coverage.

The check would send Goedert and wide receiver Jahan Dotson on a "mesh" concept running intersecting shallow crossing routes. Dotson managed to feign three Saints defenders into each other to clear plenty of space for Goedert, who caught the underneath pass and turned toward the sideline for the decisive 61-yard gain deep into Saints territory.

"I saw Jalen completely operate in chaos," coach Nick Sirianni said. "... And they executed perfectly, and then Dallas just went. He just turned it on and just went."

After the play, Goedert said he was slightly disappointed not to score. He was eventually forced out of bounds at the Saints' 4-yard line, preceding a touchdown run by Barkley on the next play to

Defensive tackle Jordan Davis sacks Saints quarterback Derek Carr during the first quarter. (Yong Kim / Staff Photographer)

give the Eagles the lead with just over a minute remaining.

"He told me if he had my speed, he would have scored, but we ended up picking it up anyway," Hurts said.

Goedert said he wasn't sure at first how he was afforded so much room when he caught the ball. It wasn't until he watched the replay on the scoreboard that he realized the significance of Dotson's contribution.

"I looked and said, 'Where is everybody?'" Goedert said. "And I ran as fast as I could as long as I could."

"I was able to see it on the replay," Goedert added when asked about Dotson's route. "I saw three people just kind of run into each other. That's what made it work. I try to do what I can do and Jahan got the big assist there. Shout-out to him because without him doing his job, I wouldn't have been able to do mine."

Finishing with two catches for 8 yards, Dotson has yet to make a sizable impact in the stat sheet since joining the Eagles via trade just before the start of the season. Still, the 24-year-old said his role in Goedert's decisive catch is an example of how he can contribute in an offense that typically features several options ahead of him in the pecking order.

Dotson also said his first few attempts at running the mesh route to spring Goedert in practice weren't nearly as effective as the one Sunday afternoon.

"It's crazy, we were running it all week because we knew they were going to play a lot of man," Dotson said. "And I wasn't running it right at the beginning of the week. Countless reps during practice, shout-out to [wide receivers coach Aaron Moorehead], he was on me about it, and we got it right in the game for two big explosives. It's really cool to be a helping hand in the game-winning play. That's kind of my role here: 'By any means necessary.' However it has to get done, I want to contribute." ∎

Tight end Dallas Goedert made an impact in Week 3, delivering a 61-yard catch and run to set up the Eagles' go-ahead touchdown. (Yong Kim / Staff Photographer)

41

SEPT. 29, 2024
TAMPA, FLA.
BUCCANEERS 33, EAGLES 16

'It Starts with Me'

Jalen Hurts falls on the sword after turnovers plague another loss

By Jeff Neiburg

Jalen Hurts pulled out his Andy Reid thesaurus and found every way possible to fall on the pirate sword after the Eagles were shot from the Raymond James Stadium cannon into their bye week with an abomination — a 33-16 defeat that felt even more lopsided and featured some of the same problems plaguing the Eagles as they limp to a 2-2 start.

Hurts used variations of "I have to be better" and "it starts with me" to answer multiple questions. The Eagles were without arguably three of their five most important offensive players in star receivers A.J. Brown and DeVonta Smith and All-Pro right tackle Lane Johnson, a caveat worth mentioning from the jump, but they again failed to score in the first quarter, becoming the only team in the NFL to be scoreless in the opening frame through four games. And Hurts again turned the ball over in a critical spot, the Eagles trailing by just two scores late in the third quarter after starting off by allowing 24 unanswered points.

The Eagles quarterback has four interceptions and three lost fumbles through four games. The Eagles are now minus-6 in the turnover department. There were more than a handful of reasons the Eagles lost Sunday, but if every other phase improves — like the defense learning to tackle and pressure the quarterback, Nick Sirianni's fourth-down decisions always being right, and if everyone were healthy — Hurts' inability to take care of the football might have them in this same position anyway.

Hurts has 27 turnovers since the beginning of the 2023 season, and no NFL quarterback has more.

Asked how he processes that reality, and what the operation will be to improve it during the bye, Hurts said: "I got to be better. That's the only thing I can say. I think things will be better once we establish an identity for ourselves, and we're trying to figure that out."

The Eagles may not have their identity yet. Tight end Dallas Goedert and running back Saquon Barkley both said after Sunday's loss that the team was still searching for one, that part of the bye week would be figuring out what that is.

Right now, their identity is a porous defense, and an offense that, led by Hurts, has nearly as many turnovers as it does touchdowns.

There's an argument to be made that Sunday's turnover wasn't on Hurts, and Sirianni made one. The Eagles had a first down at Tampa's 19-yard line trailing 30-16 inside three minutes to play in the third quarter. Hurts did well to sidestep a blitzing Lavonte David, but David got to the quarterback as he went to uncork a pass that was intended for tight end Grant Calcaterra.

"That's not Jalen, but Jalen gets credited for that," Sirianni said.

But there's an argument, too, that Hurts' pocket presence in his fifth NFL season isn't where it needs to be for a team that claims to have Super Bowl aspirations.

"I think it's a matter of being decisive and knowing exactly what you're about to do," Hurts said. "I think if we get that ball off we have an opportunity to Grant Calcaterra down the middle of the field. Just didn't end up having enough time in that situation."

Hurts, who was sacked six times, wasn't interested in using the missing players as an excuse for the offense's performance. The Eagles finished the first quarter with zero yards gained on offense. They had zero first downs to Tampa's 10. It wasn't much rosier by halftime when Tampa had 287 yards to the Eagles' 69 and 18 first downs to the Eagles' six. At one point, after rookie wide receiver Johnny Wilson left the game to be evaluated for a concussion, two of Hurts' three healthy wide receivers were practice-squad elevations Parris Campbell and John Ross.

"I didn't play good enough," Hurts said. "That's what it comes down to. Put a lot of time in this week to take advantage of this game and what we had and the guys that we had a lot of trust in. We took advantage of some and some we didn't. But, ultimately, it starts with me.

"You got to give guys opportunities and put guys in positions to be successful. I have to play point out there and distribute it, really run the show and lead it, lead the charge offensively and as a team. I got to be better at that."

After Sirianni deflected the blame from Sunday's turnover away from Hurts, he was asked about the totality of the issue, that the one constant right now has been turnovers from Hurts, who hasn't had a regular-season game without a turnover since Week 12 of last season.

"There's many things that go into it," Sirianni said. "It could be the call that we made. It could be the protection by a back or an offensive lineman. It could be somebody didn't win down the field. It could be he held onto it too long. ... At the end of the day, it's a team game and it's on all of us. To be minus-6, we all own that. All of us are responsible, starting with me."

Right now, the Eagles need less sword falling and more action. The trajectory of their season depends on it. ∎

OCT. 13, 2024
LINCOLN FINANCIAL FIELD
EAGLES 20, BROWNS 16

Grit It Out

A.J. Brown and DeVonta Smith return with TD catches in Eagles win

By Olivia Reiner

Another week, another high-drama finish for the Eagles.

Back home at Lincoln Financial Field for the first time in 27 days, the Eagles managed to keep the Cleveland Browns from pulling off a late-game comeback and emerged Sunday with a 20-16 victory. The Eagles got well over the bye week with the returns of A.J. Brown, DeVonta Smith, and Lane Johnson, whose contributions proved critical to the team's success.

Batmen return

The offense didn't get off to a strong start, even with Brown, Smith, and Johnson back in the lineup, continuing a frustrating trend for the team. The offense went three-and-out on its opening drive and failed to score in the first quarter for a fifth straight game, making the Eagles still the only team in the NFL left to do so.

However, Smith got the group going late in the first quarter. On first-and-10 from the Eagles' 22-yard line, Smith and tight end Jack Stoll ran a mesh concept that led to a 13-yard gain for the wide receiver. But the offense sputtered when Jalen Hurts' pass was batted at the line of scrimmage by Browns linebacker Jeremiah Owusu-Koramoah on third down. Smith's reception helped set up a 49-yard field

goal for Jake Elliott, giving the Eagles a 3-0 lead early in the second quarter.

Brown got in on the action on the following possession. On third-and-7 from the Browns' 22-yard line, Brown was lined up in the slot opposite cornerback Martin Emerson in man coverage. Brown ran a slot fade and was well-covered by Emerson, but Hurts placed the ball perfectly over his top receiver's back shoulder for a 22-yard touchdown to put the Eagles up, 10-0.

With eight minutes left in the game, Smith broke a 13-13 tie on yet another mesh concept with Stoll on first-and-10 from the Browns' 45. The receiver generated 40 yards after the catch and into the end zone to put the Eagles up, 20-13. He finished the game with three receptions for 64 yards and the 45-yard touchdown.

Brown racked up six receptions for 116 yards and a touchdown. His 40-yard catch on a go route down the left sideline following the two-minute warning in the fourth quarter, on a play that Hurts checked into at the line of scrimmage, put the Eagles deep in Browns territory and sealed the win. Despite his individual success, Brown acknowledged that the offense hit collective snags at times.

"I know everybody wants a game of perfection," Brown said. "But they get paid, too. They're going to

Wide receiver DeVonta Smith runs for a decisive 45-yard touchdown in the fourth quarter. (David Maialetti / Staff Photographer)

do a job trying to stop us. So that's why I'm not really too worried about it. You make adjustments as you go and, most importantly, you learn."

DeJean's first start

Coming out of the bye week, the Eagles opted to roll with rookie Cooper DeJean as the starting nickel cornerback in place of Avonte Maddox. DeJean, the team's second-round pick out of Iowa, had played only eight defensive snaps through the first four games of the season. He was far busier on Sunday, and he made the most of his newfound opportunities.

On second-and-9 from the Eagles' 49-yard line late in the first quarter, Vic Fangio sent DeJean on a blitz from the slot. Moro Ojomo was the first to break free up front, but DeJean and Bryce Huff brought down Deshaun Watson to split a sack, their first of the season. Watson was sacked five times, as

Josh Sweat, Nolan Smith, and Jalen Carter notched solo sacks and Thomas Booker and Milton Williams shared one.

DeJean was also tested in coverage. It wasn't always perfect — on the second Browns possession of the day right after they incurred a false-start penalty, Amari Cooper got open on a busted coverage for a 14-yard reception with DeJean trailing in his wake. But he also came up with a big play while the Browns attempted to make a comeback late in the fourth quarter. On first-and-goal from the 8-yard line, DeJean tackled receiver Elijah Moore short of the goal line to preserve the team's lead.

"I mean, there was a little bit of butterflies," DeJean said of his first start. "It was a lot of excitement building up to this. But once you get out there, you make that first hit, it all slows down for you. So it felt good." ■

OCT. 20, 2024
EAST RUTHERFORD, N.J.
EAGLES 28, GIANTS 3

Putting in the Work

Jalen Hurts brings calm and stabilizing presence in rout of Giants

By Mike Sielski

The best of Jalen Hurts boiled down to two plays Sunday, just two. Second quarter, fourth-and-3 from the Giants' 41-yard line. Drop back. Hang in the pocket. Take a full-frontal hit. Loft a gorgeous deep throw down the left sideline to A.J. Brown, the ball falling into Brown's hands as neatly as a coin through a soda-machine slot. A 14-point lead for the Eagles. "An aggressive play," Hurts called it later, and a vital one.

Fourth quarter. First play. Third-and-7 at the Giants' 34. Linebacker Matthew Adams bursts through the line on a blitz, a free shot at a stationary quarterback. But he slides down Hurts' left leg like a firefighter down a pole, and though his knees buckle, Hurts stays on his feet, sprints to the right, gains 16 yards and a first down. Five plays later, it's Tush Push time. Eagles 28, Giants 3. Good night, good luck, and before you exit the parking lots, make sure you sweep up the ashes of those Saquon Barkley jerseys you burned.

Two great plays. That's all. That was enough. For the second straight week, Hurts got through a game without committing a turnover, without making a throw or another decision that was befuddling in its recklessness or cluelessness, without doing anything to make it more difficult for the Eagles to beat an opponent they should beat nine times out of 10. When a quarterback has the kind of season Hurts had two years ago, when he outplays Patrick Mahomes in a performance worthy of winning the Super Bowl MVP Award, when he and his team agree to a contract extension that could pay him as much as $255 million, the great plays usually cease to be surprising. People figure they're going to see them and see them often. They become the expectation.

"You want to be able to win in multiple ways," Hurts said, "and I think as we continue to build, we'll continue to see that even more. That's what the good offenses have. They're capable of doing both. They're not one-dimensional.

"Everybody knows what kind of ball we're capable of playing. That's why we're held to that standard [by] everyone. So that reality is, you just need to continue to climb."

He was correct all around. There is a standard for Hurts and the Eagles, and maybe now, nearly five years into his career with them, it's time to adjust that standard. To lower it some. He was excellent

Jalen Hurts had a modest day through the air with 114 yards and a touchdown but was dangerous on the ground, adding two more touchdowns in the easy win. (David Maialetti / Staff Photographer)

last week against the Browns, maybe the best part of an otherwise unimpressive game from the Eagles offense, and he was clean and efficient and wasn't called on to do too much against the Giants: 10-for-14, 114 passing yards — 89 of which went to one guy, Brown — a couple of QB-sneak TDs.

Mostly, his day's assignment was basic: Don't make a crushing and inexcusable mistake. Give the ball to Barkley. Get out of the way.

"He's just really emphasized the things he wanted to work on and that we needed to work on for the success of the team," coach Nick Sirianni said. "That's something about Jalen Hurts: Anything that he feels or we feel or anybody feels that we need to get better at, he's going to work his butt off to do so. I really admire him for that."

He should. For all the tension that appears to be simmering beneath Hurts' sometimes-cryptic public comments about his head coach, each benefits from the other's presence. Though, compared to last week's postgame press conference, he was notably more subdued Sunday, Sirianni generally speaks and carries himself as if he has an electric cable crackling through him, never more so than over the last two weeks. Hurts grounds him. He has been and should continue to be the Eagles' stabilizing force, accepting and filling the role of the mature leader of the team.

As the franchise quarterback, Hurts has the power and leverage in his relationship with Sirianni, and he often speaks as if he knows it. He did Sunday.

"Obviously, he knows I'm behind him," Hurts said. "He knows that communication is important amongst a team sport, and he's been doing a good job. He's really come in with good intensity, good intentionality, trying to deliver good messages for

us to be focused and be on the same page. He's also apologetic when he needs to be."

That's as strong a defense of Sirianni as Hurts has ever delivered, and it's a long time coming. There have been occasions when he has seemed hesitant to praise him, to stand up for his coach in the same way Sirianni has always stood up for him, especially during that string of nine straight games when Hurts couldn't stop throwing interceptions or losing fumbles.

Sunday was better. Sunday was calmer for Sirianni and cleaner for Hurts. Sunday was the most one-sided Eagles victory in more than a year. None of that is coincidental. Two great plays and solid, smooth, error-free football from Jalen Hurts. That's all. That's the proper standard now. ∎

Saquon Barkley ran wild in his return to MetLife Stadium to face his former team, destroying the Giants with 17 carries for 176 yards and a touchdown. (David Maialetti / Staff Photographer)

OCT. 27, 2024
CINCINNATI, OHIO
EAGLES 37, BENGALS 17

Forward Motion

DeVonta Smith's TD catch underscores a bounce-back day against the Bengals

By EJ Smith

I t was late in the first quarter when the intrusive thoughts won over in DeVonta Smith's head.

We ain't doing this again.

In the early going of the Eagles' dominant 37-17 win over the Cincinnati Bengals, the wide receiver was thrown down for a 2-yard loss on his first catch of the day. He had plenty of time to amend the broken play, but the stat line looked all too familiar. One catch, minus-2 yards.

Smith had been a good sport a week earlier when his limited role in a blowout win against the Giants resulted in the same exact numbers. The Eagles' history of overcorrecting to a quiet game from one of their stars the last few years even suggested Smith would be featured early and often this Sunday, but the 25-year-old finished the opening series with a similar lack of involvement, an identical stat sheet, and a determination to avoid another week of going backward.

"Today, I wasn't happy when that happened," Smith said of his opening catch. "I was like, 'Nah, we ain't doing this again.' But it's just trusting my training, continuing to go out there and make the most of my opportunities. When the ball comes to you, make it."

Smith did just that, making an improbable contested catch for a 45-yard touchdown that proved instrumental in the Eagles cruising to their most convincing win of the season. Finishing with six catches for a team-high 85 receiving yards and the score, the star wideout made a handful of timely plays to help the Eagles convert on third downs during the second half as well.

After the game, Eagles coach Nick Sirianni alluded to the offense's tendency to feature Smith, A.J. Brown, or Dallas Goedert heavily the week after a quiet game. He didn't get the numbers exactly right — Smith had eight catches for 169 yards and a touchdown in Week 3 of the 2022 season against the Washington Commanders two games after having zero catches against the Lions — but the sentiment holds true. Smith has never gone consecutive games with fewer than four targets and has typically followed up his worst statistical performances with big games the following week.

"He made clutch catches," Sirianni said. "Not a surprise, the last time he was shut out in a game — he had one for minus-2 last week — but the last time he was shut out in a game he came back and had, I

DeVonta Smith (6) bounced back after a tough game a week earlier against the Giants with six catches for 85 yards and a touchdown in the win over the Bengals. (David Maialetti / Staff Photographer)

The Philadelphia Inquirer

think, like eight for 176. That's how the game goes, that's why you can't overreact when things happen."

Eagles quarterback Jalen Hurts added, "We've got a lot of talent, we've got a lot of mouths to feed. That's something that we have to navigate as a team, but the one thing I'm confident in is everyone being ready when their opportunity and their number is called. He made some huge plays down the stretch of the game down the field, and then on third downs he showed up big. I think that was a great showing for him and a great showing for our offense and our team."

Smith's biggest play came late in the third quarter with the score tied at 17. The Eagles identified zone coverage by motioning tight end Jack Stoll across the formation and called a play-action deep shot that sent Smith and Brown on routes down the field. Isolated against Cincinnati safety Jordan Battle, Smith gained some separation but still needed to high-point the ball with Battle scrambling to recover.

"We knew we were going to get the one-on-one coverage," Smith said. "Jalen, he trusted me to go up there, one-on-one, and win a 50-50 ball."

Sparked by the big play, the Eagles went on to score 20 unanswered points with Smith contributing two critical third-down catches to help the offense salt the game away.

The touchdown catch is the type of play Smith has developed a reputation for during his Eagles tenure despite having a slender frame. He said he hadn't watched the catch back after the game, so he

wasn't sure where it may rank among his best plays over the last few years.

Brown, Smith's running mate, said his vantage point was good enough to confirm it will rank highly.

"It's up there," Brown said. "I got a live view. It's up there."

There's an irony in Smith adding to his highlight reel so emphatically just one week after his most impactful plays came blocking for Saquon Barkley at MetLife Stadium. That wasn't lost on him as he walked toward the podium shortly after the final whistle with "September" blaring through a jubilant Eagles locker room and competing with his voice in an adjacent room.

"I ain't done one of these in a while." ■

Cornerback Darius Slay Jr. (2) helped limit receiver Jermaine Burton (81) and Cincinnati's explosive offense to just 17 points in the blowout win. (Monica Herndon / Staff Photographer)

53

NOV. 3, 2024
LINCOLN FINANCIAL FIELD
EAGLES 28, JAGUARS 23

'The Best Play I've Ever Seen'

Saquon Barkley cements his role as centerpiece of the Eagles offense

By Jeff McLane

There were no words to describe what Saquon Barkley had done. Even the most apt and immediate description — "a backward hurdle" — couldn't do it justice. A video replay on loop fails to capture his athletically freakish feat.

You just had to be there.

Sure, millions watched Barkley moonleap — better, but not quite — over Jacksonville Jaguars cornerback Jarrian Jones on live television. But to see the running back spontaneously pull it off in person, to hear the reaction from fans at Lincoln Financial Field, and to glimpse the exuberance of the Eagles sideline was a moment that could only be captured in the mind's eye.

Barkley had done something no one had even done before and it was almost all for naught. The Eagles nearly coughed up a 22-point lead to the hapless Jaguars, but few will remember an eventual 28-23 win on Sunday years from now. It was that uninspiring.

What will last was Barkley's superhuman no-look hurdle. It defied description. He attributed it to divine intervention and, well, why not?

"I got to give credit to God, I'm not going to lie," Barkley said. "I feel like — not in a cocky way — I do believe God blessed me. He blesses all of us. But I feel like God gave me an ability to play this position and gave me some instincts.

"Sometimes you got to let go and let God and your instincts take over."

Eagles coach Nick Sirianni has taken a similar approach with his offense since the bye. He has let go of the idea of having a pass-heavy attack led by quarterback Jalen Hurts and has let Barkley and the run game take over.

Hurts will be elemental to the Eagles' success or failure, of course. He's been more efficient during the current four-game winning streak, and there will come a time when his arm will have to shoulder the load. The quarterback position is just too vital in the modern NFL for it to be secondary.

But Barkley has become the centerpiece of the Eagles offense. On Sunday, he rushed 27 times for 159 yards and a touchdown and caught three passes for 40 yards and another score.

Barkley is averaging only two more touches per game in the last four games vs. the first four. But the Eagles have emphasized having more of a run-heavy offense — with backup running

Saquon Barkley pulled off one of the most audacious and incredible moves in NFL history with a backward hurdle over Jacksonville cornerback Jarrian Jones. (Yong Kim / Staff Photographer)

back Kenneth Gainwell also getting more carries — after offensive linemen Lane Johnson, Jordan Mailata, and Landon Dickerson pushed for it over the last month.

"I want to [bleeping] win," Dickerson said when asked why they went to Sirianni and offensive coordinator Kellen Moore. "Simple as that. Whatever it takes to win."

In this narrative, Sirianni and Moore get credit for being open to change. But they obviously knew something had to change after the Eagles opened the season 2-2 with Hurts having seven turnovers.

The overall run-pass ratio since the bye tilts heavily in favor of the run. But those numbers can be a little misleading because the Eagles held double-digit leads over the New York Giants and Cincinnati Bengals the previous two weeks.

The first-half disparity between the run-pass ratio in the first four games (34% to 66%) vs. the last four (48% to 52%) shows how Moore's play-calling has been committed to establishing the ground game. And while it has taken a quarter to get moving at times, or it hasn't always looked pretty, the results have spoken for themselves.

"Barkley is a big reason. Kenny's a big reason," Dickerson said. "Jalen on the read options — big reason. There's a lot of reasons why. But if it works, ain't no reason to mess with it."

In the first four games, Hurts averaged 39 drops per game. In the last four, he's averaged just 26 drops. He deserves accolades for not having a turnover since the bye. He's had some amazing throws and runs over that period.

Against the Jaguars, Hurts completed 18 of 24 passes for 230 yards and two touchdowns and rushed 13 times for 67 yards and a touchdown. He wasn't perfect. He missed some receivers and some throws and took a few unnecessary sacks.

But the Eagles' current formula is one that doesn't revolve the offense almost entirely around Hurts. Barkley has as much to do with that as anything.

"We knew he was special," Sirianni said. "I think when you're around him on a daily basis it's safe to say, yes, that he's even more special than I could have even imagined."

Barkley has had his sloppy moments this season, as well. There was the dropped pass late in the Atlanta Falcons loss. There was a run out of bounds short of the sticks against the Cleveland Browns. He had another drop against the Jaguars, and his third-quarter fumble — however dubious the call — brought the Jaguars back into the picture.

"No excuses. I got to be better in that situation," Barkley said. "That play kind of sparked Jacksonville."

A slide short of the sticks during the four-minute offense could have also cost the Eagles. But Barkley did so many positives things that a few errors can be forgotten.

There was an over-the-shoulder catch for a 20-yard touchdown. There was a 19-yard touchdown run on a third-and-17 draw. There were carries when Barkley motored into the Jaguars secondary. And there were countless rushes when he picked up yards after contact.

But it was his second-quarter catch on third-and-6 – which simply reads, "J.Hurts pass short left to S.Barkley to JAX 30 for 14 yards" on the stat sheet — that will live in memories and on career highlight reels for decades to come.

Even before his hurdle, he broke cornerback Tyson Campbell's tackle attempt. He then spun away from linebacker Devin Lloyd. Barkley could have just let himself get tackled with the first down secured and his back to the Jaguars defense. It was probably the safe play.

But he elevated, separated his legs, and vaulted over the diving Jones.

Saquon Barkley's acrobatics against the Jaguars produced 27 carries for 159 yards and a touchdown, as well as three catches for 40 yards and another trip to the end zone. (Yong Kim / Staff Photographer)

"It was the best play I've ever seen," Sirianni said.

Barkley pulled off something similar as a Penn State sophomore. "But it wasn't as cool," he said. During the summer, he said he told safety C.J. Gardner-Johnson and cornerback Kelee Ringo that he might try it again in the NFL.

Once may be enough. The Eagles can't afford to lose their workhorse. He doesn't have as many touches through eight games as he did two years ago with the Giants. But Barkley, who needs just 75 yards to eclipse 1,000 on the ground for the season, is on pace for a career-high 333 carries.

"My body feels good," he said. "I kind of got banged up a little bit today. Not gonna get too into what happened. Nothing crazy, just a little TLC this week, and I'll be ready to go."

And everyone else will be there to watch in speechless awe. ∎

NOV. 10, 2024
ARLINGTON, TEXAS
EAGLES 34, COWBOYS 6

'A Lot of History Here'

Jalen Hurts and Jalen Carter lead humiliation of Cowboys

By Marcus Hayes

Less than 30 minutes into the game, the Eagles were trying to give the game away to the Dallas Cowboys. Less than 15 minutes later, the game was effectively over.

Jalen Hurts continued his smooth play of the past four games through the first quarter, but then he committed a pair of unforgivable turnovers after a four-game streak without any. But in the matter of two minutes, defensive tackle Jalen Carter minimized the damage of the second turnover with a big tackle for loss, Hurts regained his composure, and the Eagles were on their way to ending a six-game losing streak at AT&T Stadium with a 34-6 win.

"Those moments were probably the biggest part of the game," said Saquon Barkley, who's been the biggest part of the Eagles' season. "We don't know how the game goes after that. We definitely stopped their momentum. They get a turnover but don't score a touchdown. Then we go score a touchdown. That's an 11-point swing."

Carter and the Eagles defense remained stingy. It has allowed fewer than 11 points per game (not counting a fumble return and a special-teams TD) since the bye. It forced five turnovers Sunday, but did so against a toothless, leaderless offense. It was a rather pathetic showing from the hosts, who couldn't capitalize on Hurts' worst moments in months.

You almost pitied the Cowboys, a franchise whose self-aggrandizement has, for almost 30 years, far outstripped its self-competence. Now 3-6, Jerry's world continued to crumble, and you almost felt sorry for them.

Almost.

Meanwhile, as the Eagles surged to 7-2 and first place in the NFC East with a fifth straight win, the Cowboys, the preseason division favorites, suffered a fifth straight loss with no help in sight. Dak Prescott, their $240 million quarterback, has a torn hamstring and missed the first of what might be eight games — or, for all intents and purposes, the rest of the season. His replacement, Cooper Rush, remains a poor substitute. Other injuries and deficiencies to the Cowboys and the garbage barge that is the New York Giants, now 2-8, have made the East a two-team race. The upstart Commanders lost Sunday and fell to 7-3, so the upcoming Thursday Night Football in Philly now carries far more weight

Safety C.J. Gardner-Johnson intercepts a pass from Cowboys quarterback Trey Lance in the fourth quarter. (Monica Herndon / Staff Photographer)

than schedulers anticipated when they made it a throwaway game on Prime Video.

What ended as the springboard for more questions about the future of Dallas coach Mike McCarthy, who should have been fired months ago, began with a series of Eagles catastrophes, authored mainly by Hurts.

On the first play of the second quarter, Hurts threw an end-zone interception toward Dallas Goedert, who wasn't open and who was running into double coverage. Hurts seemed to enter a haze of confusion.

On the ensuing drive he took two bad sacks and, in between, burned a timeout to avoid a delay-of-game penalty. The Birds punted, but Ezekiel Elliott fumbled into the end zone, which gave the Birds the ball back deep in their own territory, but Hurts remained hesitant.

Micah Parsons strip-sacked Hurts, who'd failed to tuck the ball away when contact was imminent, which gave the Cowboys the ball at the Eagles' 6. A TD seemed inevitable.

Then, two plays later, on third-and-goal from the 3, Carter showed up.

Carter grabbed guard Cooper Beebe by the "5" and "6" on his jersey, threw him aside like a trash bag, and drove straight into Rico Dowdle for a 2-yard loss and forced a field goal that preserved a 7-6 lead.

"There's times we've got to save the defense's ass," said Barkley, "and times when they've got to save our ass."

The Eagles offense got the ball back with 1 minute, 43 seconds to play in the half, and Hurts found himself again.

Hurts feathered a 14-yard out pattern to A.J. Brown on the right sideline, hit DeVonta Smith on a 5-yard quickie in the same direction, then underthrew Smith on a blitz-buster deep pass. No worries.

On third-and-5, again facing a blitz, Hurts waited an extra beat for Brown to cross his face, right-to-left, over the middle; 18 yards. The Cowboys called off the dogs and Hurts scrambled for 24, dumped a hesitation route to third-down back Kenneth Gainwell that made it second-and-1 at the Cowboys' 14. They blitzed again, but Hurts saw it, evaded (and maybe even baited) linebacker DeMarvion Overshown, rolled right and hit tight end Goedert at the goal line for a 14-6 halftime lead.

How did Hurts turn it around?

"One of the hardest things to do is just move on," said Nick Sirianni, the Eagles' head coach and chief philosopher. "He moved on. That's what winners do."

"You treat every play as its own," Hurts said.

This game was different. Hurts is a Texas native, and he'd entered the game with an 80.9 passer rating and an 0-3 record in three visits to Jerry's World. Sunday, his passer rating was 115.0. He'd done it under the guidance of offensive coordinator Kellen Moore, the former Cowboys backup QB and former offensive coordinator that Jerry Jones fired as the scapegoat for the Cowboys' 2022 postseason collapse. It had been a long time since other players, like Texas native Lane Johnson and avowed Cowboys hater Brandon Graham, had left Big D happy.

"I think we all have a lot of history here," Hurts said.

They've begun writing a new chapter by — as usual — not trying to do too much.

At his best, Hurts does no harm, and that's how the third quarter began, with a conservative three-and-out from the Eagles, a 31-yard punt return from Cooper DeJean, which set up a cool, seven-play, 37-yard TD drive, punctuated by a 5-yard touchdown pass to Johnny Wilson, on which Hurts had seven unmolested seconds to throw.

Hurts hit Brown for 44 yards to start the next drive and ended it with an 8-yard QB TD keeper, and, at 28-6, everybody in Arlington began planning the rest of their evening.

Saquon Barkley had to carry the ball only 14 times for 66 yards in the comfortable 34-6 win over the division rival Cowboys. (Monica Herndon / Staff Photographer)

Hurts played one more series before Kenny Pickett replaced him. Hurts finished 14-for-20 for 202 passing yards with two touchdowns and an interception, as well as two rushing TDs. It was his fifth straight game with a passer rating over 100. He had none in the first four games of the season, when the team was 2-2.

Similarly, Carter continued his post-bye binge. He added a half-sack to his three others this season, hit Rush twice, and had that key tackle for

loss. With the retirement of Fletcher Cox, Carter, in his second season, remains the defense's most significant player.

Sunday, he made the most significant play.

"It was real big," Carter agreed. "Let them just kick a field goal. Three points is better than six points, right?"

Yep.

Every time. ∎

NOV. 14, 2024
LINCOLN FINANCIAL FIELD
EAGLES 26, COMMANDERS 18

Don't You Worry 'Bout a Thing

Saquon Barkley, Vic Fangio's defense take down the Commanders

By Jeff Neiburg

Stevie Wonder was playing in a happy Eagles locker room late Thursday night, and Saquon Barkley had just enough time before encroaching reporters reached his locker stall to sing a line from the chorus.

Don't you worry 'bout a thing, Barkley sang softly.

It was the story of the night. It is the story of the season. With Barkley, the Eagles don't have to worry about a thing.

For 45-plus minutes, the Eagles were doing just about everything better than Washington except in the only category that matters — the scoreboard. They were dominating in yards gained. Their defense was stingy. If not for missed Jake Elliott kicks, poor red-zone play, and shaky decision making from Jalen Hurts, the Eagles would have been leading.

Then the running game finally showed its force. The Eagles' go-ahead drive started on their own 24-yard line late in the third quarter with a 9-yard Barkley run. It featured carries from Kenneth Gainwell of 14, 13, and 7 yards. Barkley's 3-yard run put the Eagles at the 1-yard line, and they pushed their quarterback over the goal line on the next play. Then, after the defense forced a turnover on downs, Barkley put the game away.

Hurts hit Dallas Goedert for a 32-yard gain to push the Eagles onto Washington's side of the field. Three plays later, on a third-and-3 from the 23-yard line, Barkley took a shotgun handoff from Hurts and ran to his right, burst through a big hole created by Lane Johnson, and was off to the races to put the Eagles up two scores with 4 minutes, 58 seconds to play.

Twenty seconds later, after a Reed Blankenship interception, the game was over. Hurts, taking a snap from under center, tossed the ball to Barkley, who started to his right and then cut to his left and went 39 yards untouched into the end zone.

He dropped the ball in the end zone — nearly before he reached the plane, he admitted later — put his arms out and sprinted to the Eagles sideline, a two-game lead in the loss column in the vapor trail behind him.

"That's the beauty of football," Barkley said. "You can stop us for 20-something carries, but when you rip off two long ones when it matters most, the stats look pretty good and most times you get a win."

Barkley's final stat line was 146 yards on 26 carries and two scores, the sixth time he has topped 100 yards in 10 games this season. He eclipsed the 1,000-yard mark for the fourth time in his career, and

Saquon Barkley had plenty to celebrate in the win over the Commanders with 26 carries for 146 yards and two touchdowns. (Monica Herndon / Staff Photographer)

the Eagles still have seven games to play. Barkley added 52 yards on a pair of catches, including a 43-yard catch and run midway through the third quarter to extend a drive that ended with the Eagles cutting a 10-3 deficit to 10-6.

Take away those two long touchdown scores, though, and Barkley's right. It was just 84 yards on 24 carries, a per-carry average of 3.5 yards. It was a frustrating first half for a pass-happy offense. Hurts struggled to find open receivers, and Eagles rushers infrequently found room to run. The Eagles had three points at halftime, in part because of two Elliott misses.

The Eagles had some tinkering to do. Washington, left guard Landon Dickerson said, made pregame adjustments to the Eagles, and now the Eagles had to respond with some of their own. What were they? "Why would I tell you that? I'm not giving you grandma's secret recipe," Dickerson said.

Johnson was slightly more forthcoming. "We had some plays that we saved and didn't run the first half that we did a good job of hitting on in the second half," he said. Barkley credited run game coordinator and offensive line coach Jeff Stoutland and running backs coach Jemal Singleton with making some changes at halftime.

"We don't panic," Barkley said. "We trust in each other. We know one of us, somebody, is going to make a play. In the running game, we felt like we were one read off or one block off."

Jordan Mailata, back from a hamstring injury, had a simpler explanation: "I think it was just will," he said. "I think you have to want it more than the other team."

The simplest answer, though, is that the Eagles have Barkley. The Eagles are 8-2, and it's hard to imagine they'd be anywhere near six games above .500

if they hadn't opted to sign Barkley in the offseason.

Hard to imagine, too, that they would be on this six-game winning streak had Johnson, Dickerson, and Mailata not gone to Nick Sirianni to implore the coach to help the Eagles get back to their running ways. The Eagles ran the ball 40 times Thursday night. They have run it more than 40 times per game during their winning streak. A few of those games have been blowouts, and you run the ball when you're winning big, but they're winning big in part because they're running the ball.

"When we get the running game going, it's kind of hard to beat our team," Barkley said. "But the beauty of that is we have a lot of other great talent on this team, too. We've got to find ways to continue to get them involved and keep taking it one game at a time."

A sound approach, but recent results have shown that it all starts with him. Barkley has been the X factor, one who, especially on Thursday night, can change everything.

"It makes you look a lot better than maybe what you are," Johnson quipped about Barkley's presence.

"I knew the guy was a special player," Mailata said. "The what-ifs, the possibilities of what he could do behind our offensive line, you don't really know what to expect until you see it, until he does something. Special player, man. I'm glad he's on our side."

While the result was still in question Thursday night, Mailata turned to Barkley and said: "I'll be damned if we lose this game in my comeback game."

Barkley, Mailata said, responded: "I got you."

Later, after he delivered on his words, Barkley found Mailata. "I told you," he said.

He could have just sung Stevie's lyrics. ■

Commanders quarterback Jayden Daniels is sacked by Eagles defensive end Brandon Graham (obscured) and defensive tackle Milton Williams (right) during the win over Washington. (Monica Herndon / Staff Photographer)

NOV. 24, 2024
INGLEWOOD, CALIF.
EAGLES 37, RAMS 20

'We're Not Satisfied'

With dismantling of Rams, Eagles set their sights on the Super Bowl

By Mike Sielski

The Eagles have reached the point that most NFL teams aspire to and only the best of the best can handle with the right combination of confidence and care.

They are 9-2 now after their 37-20 victory over the Los Angeles Rams at SoFi Stadium. They seized control of the game in the second quarter — against a team that had been rolling, that had won four of its previous five games — and never let go. They have pulled away from the other three teams in the NFC East, one of which (the Washington Commanders) isn't ready yet to win consistently and two of which (the New York Giants and Dallas Cowboys) are piles of offal. They are at worst the second-best team in the conference; only the Detroit Lions are superior, and the distance between the two teams would depend on whether they were facing each other at Ford Field or Lincoln Financial Field.

They have Saquon Barkley, who has been the best running back — perhaps the best player, period — in the league this season. It would be correct to say that watching Barkley run is like watching water flow over rocks ... except to capture the full feeling of watching Barkley, the water would also have to flow around the rocks and through the air and from side to side. Barkley rushed for 255 yards and two touchdowns — both of which were at least 70 yards — against the Rams. John Mara, the owner of the franchise that Barkley used to play for, must have been sick.

The Eagles have A.J. Brown, who is perhaps the best wide receiver in the league. They have an offensive line that is as good as any in the league. They have Vic Fangio overseeing their defense and Kellen Moore overseeing their offense, coordinators who are savvy and experienced and whose units have been improving gradually week by week. They have Nick Sirianni, a head coach for whom the phrase "He must be doing something right" had to have been invented. Under him, the Eagles do a lot of things that make you shake your head, but the thing they do most of all is win.

"Everyone's going to be telling us how good we are," Sirianni said. "Everyone's going to be telling us, 'You're one of the better teams.' We don't listen to that. All we've got to do is put our heads down and work. It's just like when people tell you that you aren't good enough and you've got to block it out and put your head down and work. It's the same situation

Running back Kenneth Gainwell celebrates his third-quarter touchdown with wide receiver A.J. Brown during the Eagles' 37-20 win over the Rams. (David Maialetti / Staff Photographer)

here. What's going to happen, obviously — and this is what I told our team after — is everyone's going to be calling you. The media's going to be telling you how good you are. That all doesn't matter. All that matters is we go back to work."

The Eagles have plugged two rookies into their secondary, Quinyon Mitchell and Cooper DeJean, and a former pass rusher in at linebacker, Zack Baun, and the defense has been terrific for seven straight games now. They have Jalen Hurts, a quarterback who apparently has decided that committing a turnover is the worst of all outcomes for him and his team and who is going out of his way to not commit one. Given the talent around him, given the benefits of being a team that simply doesn't mess up as often as its opponents do, that's not the worst approach.

"You've got to remember what wins games, and a lot of it is how you handle Wednesday, Thursday, Friday practices," right tackle Lane Johnson said. "All that stuff can translate to the game on Sunday. It's not just 'Show up and play and win.' There's a lot of stuff that goes into the process to win games. If you have good, clean, crisp practices, if you preach, 'Don't turn over the ball,' if you preach taking away the ball and playing physical, some of that stuff sounds redundant when you're listening to it, but it's really what it boils down to. Anybody can knock you on your ass — if you don't have everything detailed.

"I want to remember what wins games, and it's the week. It's Wednesdays and Thursdays when you feel like [expletive] and you don't want to do anything. That's what wins games."

What this bounty of riches means is simple: The Eagles are a contender and should be evaluated as such, because they will judge themselves by that standard. Anything less than an appearance in Super Bowl LIX ought to be regarded as a disappointment. Anything less than an appearance in the NFC championship game ought to be regarded as a failure. That's the point they've reached. That's the way to look at them. They were at this point two years ago, when they were one half away from the second Super Bowl victory in their history. They are at this point again.

"We're not satisfied," Hurts said. "We weren't satisfied in the past, and we're not satisfied now."

The Rams are no pushover. They have a Hall of Fame quarterback in Matthew Stafford and two game-breaking receivers in Cooper Kupp and Puka Nacua and one of the NFL's sharpest minds in coach Sean McVay. And the Eagles tore them apart. A performance like this one, against an opponent like this one, raises the stakes. The standard is established. Let's see if they can maintain this excellence and meet it. ■

Saquon Barkley rushed for 255 yards and two touchdowns as the Eagles improved 9-2 on the season. (Yong Kim / Staff Photographer)

'Meant to Be'

Saquon Barkley authors MVP-level performance in Eagles' romp over Rams

By Olivia Reiner | Nov. 25, 2024

Fresh off his 302-scrimmage-yard heroics against the Los Angeles Rams, Saquon Barkley returned to the visitors locker room at SoFi Stadium and encountered a familiar sight — a request for a drug test.

The half sheet of paper that hung from the top shelf of Barkley's stall has become as commonplace as the "No. 26" nameplate affixed above it. However, upon further inspection, the Eagles' star running back noticed the name "D. Goedert" scrawled at the top of the sheet. Dallas Goedert had pulled a prank on Barkley, removing his own drug test notice from his stall and taping it to his teammate's in the aftermath of his historic night.

"I've been drug tested enough," Barkley deadpanned. "Hopefully I get away from that for a little bit."

Barkley's seemingly supernatural season with the Eagles came to a crescendo in Sunday's win, as the 27-year-old running back burned the Rams defense on the ground for a single-game career-best 255 rushing yards and two touchdowns on 26 carries. He set the franchise record for rushing yards in a game, besting LeSean McCoy's 217-yard performance in 2013.

Thanks to the litany of statistics featured on the gigantic infinity loop-style scoreboard dangling from the roof of the stadium, Barkley had a sense of how close he was to breaking his previous personal best of 189 rushing yards. He looked up at the screen after the Eagles' first possession of the fourth quarter and noticed his counter stuck at 173.

"I literally said to myself, 'I wish I never saw that,' because that's just the devil talking," Barkley said. "That's just how I look at it. Just kept my head down and just kept trusting the system and we popped a long one."

After a relatively slow start in the first half (73 yards on 13 carries), a pair of explosive touchdown runs in the second accounted for nearly half of Barkley's damage on the ground and put him well above his previous personal best.

The first touchdown came on the first play of the Eagles' second-half opening possession. After navigating through a lane created by Landon Dickerson and Cam Jurgens on an outside zone run to the first-down marker, Barkley planted his left foot in the turf and cut toward the sideline with his right, gaining leverage on Rams safety Kamren Kinchens, who had crashed. Following the game, Nick Sirianni called it a cut that he didn't think anybody else could make.

Barkley took off outside the numbers and crossed the goal line unscathed for a 70-yard touchdown run to put the Eagles up two scores, 20-7. In the locker room, the running back credited the efforts of the offensive line for making his job easier. The offensive line reciprocated that acknowledgment.

Eagles single-season rushing leaders

PLAYER	YEAR	YDS	ATT	AVG	TD
LeSean McCoy	2013	1,607	314	5.1	9
Wilbert Montgomery	1979	1,512	338	4.5	9
Saquon Barkley	**2024**	**1,499**	**246**	**6.1**	**11**
Ricky Watters	1996	1,411	353	4.0	13
Wilbert Montgomery	1981	1,402	286	4.9	8

Table: Rob Tornoe – Source: NFL data

"He's an absolute stud," Jurgens said. "I freakin' love blocking for that guy. I think he loves running for us. You've just got to do your own job and just got to get a little bit of a piece on the linebacker, the D-lineman. Just a little bit extra, 'cause he's ready to spring any run."

Barkley wasn't finished. Late in the fourth quarter with the Eagles looking to close out the game, Kellen Moore dialed up a "counter" run concept in which Grant Calcaterra pulled across the formation to block for Barkley. The running back said that it was a similar play to one that the Eagles had attempted earlier in the game, but his cleat had come off when he was tackled.

The play had a different fate the second time around. Calcaterra sealed off Rams safety Kam Curl on the edge, allowing Barkley to cut behind the tight end and burst through the hole downfield. Barkley cruised into the end zone on a 72-yard touchdown run to seal the victory and his numerous milestones.

His night ended after the TD run, earning the ninth-highest total of scrimmage yards (255 rushing, 47 receiving) in a game by any player in NFL history. If Barkley wasn't already among the front-runners for the league's most valuable player accolade, his performance might as well have been a formal application.

Despite the "MVP" chants from the throngs of Eagles fans who made the trip to Los Angeles that inundated Barkley as he ran off the field, postseason awards aren't on the running back's mind yet.

"We'll start thinking about that when the season's over," Barkley said. "I love being in that conversation. It's cool and all. But like I said, it's a team sport. If you tell me that I could have the year I'm having and win an MVP but not win a Super Bowl or I can have the year I'm having and not win MVP or offensive player of the year and win a Super Bowl, I'm going to take the other one."

Nearly 3,000 miles east of the site where Barkley made franchise history with his 302 all-purpose yards, his former New York Giants team amassed just 245 yards of total offense in a loss to the Tampa Bay Buccaneers at MetLife Stadium.

When Barkley left the Giants after six seasons to sign a three-year deal with the Eagles in the offseason, he said he didn't know if he could have this much success. The supporting cast around him — including Lane Johnson, A.J. Brown, and Jalen Hurts — has encouraged Barkley to make plays and "do something special" in Philadelphia.

"I think this is a spot where I can kind of rewrite my story," Barkley said. "I feel like I can show everyone the type of player that I feel like I can be and was meant to be."

Two explosive touchdown runs, 302 historic scrimmage yards, and a drug-test prank later, Barkley isn't finished writing his latest chapter with the Eagles.

"My story's not finished and it's going to keep going," he said. ■

DEC. 1, 2024
BALTIMORE
EAGLES 24, RAVENS 19

'The Energy is There'

Even with reduced manpower, Eagles make statement with win over Ravens

By Marcus Hayes

Jalen Hurts committed no turnovers, Saquon Barkley gained 107 rushing yards and scored the decisive touchdown, the defense shut down the NFL's top offense, and the Eagles left Baltimore with an eighth straight win.

Now they are 10-2 and there can be no more debate. No more doubt.

The Eagles are a Super Bowl-caliber team. They beat you up. They beat you down. They beat you, period.

"I feel like the energy is there. We're building momentum," said Lane Johnson, who won Super Bowl LII with the Eagles and went back five years later. "But you remember last year."

Last year, the Eagles started 10-1 but lost five of their last six games and got blown out of the playoffs in Tampa. So what.

"Last year's over," said coach Nick Sirianni. "We don't care about last year. This is a different team that's jelling and meshing on all cylinders right now."

They stifled the No. 1 offense; the Ravens entered the game averaging 6.97 yards per play over 12 games, which ranked second in NFL history ... by one-hundredth of a point, to the legendary 2000 St. Louis Rams, the Greatest Show on Turf. The Eagles allowed 5.24 yards per play, and before they gifted the Ravens a touchdown with three seconds to play, they'd allowed them 4.72 yards per play.

The Birds ran all over the No. 2 run defense, which was allowing just 77.9 yards per game; they had 140. Reigning MVP Lamar Jackson, a current MVP favorite, looked pedestrian. Derrick "King" Henry, the league's No. 2 rusher behind Barkley, managed just 82 yards, having averaged 110.4.

Ravens star kicker Justin Tucker continued his nightmare season with two more missed field goals and a missed extra point, but the 24-19 final score and the reality of Sunday's exhibition muted his miscues.

There was no question: The Eagles were the superior team — the more physical team — with the emphasis on team.

Sirianni bristled at the idea that the Eagles needed to match the Ravens' toughness. It was the other way around.

"That was the message going in: They've got to match our physicality," Sirianni said.

Everybody played a part. They came back from a 9-0 first-quarter deficit. They didn't flinch. Championship teams don't.

A.J. Brown reacts after a catch and run against the Baltimore Ravens in the second quarter. The Eagles offense found its stride to overcome an early deficit. (Monica Herndon / Staff Photographer)

Offensive coordinator Kellen Moore solved the Ravens' scheme by the second quarter and had Hurts find A.J. Brown in the defense's soft midsection.

Defensive coordinator Vic Fangio, plagued by manpower issues, patched together a scheme that gave up just 10 points after the first quarter.

Hurts was 11-for-19 for just 118 yards, but that's all he needed.

Barkley didn't break any big ones, but he did collect an 11th TD, from 25 yards out, midway through the fourth quarter.

And the defense? Chef's kiss.

Star tackle Jalen Carter had a sack and now has 4½. Rookie end Jalyx Hunt, playing in place of injured Brandon Graham, got a half-sack, and now has 1½ in his career.

In the middle of the second quarter, Jordan Davis stopped Henry for a 1-yard gain. Two plays later, linebacker Zack Baun dropped Henry for a 4-yard loss. In the middle of the fourth quarter, Carter stuffed Henry for a 1-yard loss, Cooper DeJean stoned him for a meager 3-yard gain, and backup safety Tristin McCollum unintentionally, but fortunately, knocked down a fourth-down pass (an interception would have meant worse field position). That set up a field goal.

They're a Tush Push team, and they cannot be stopped. They got a Tush Push touchdown in the second quarter for a 14-12 halftime lead. They got a Tush Push fourth-down conversion late in the fourth quarter to burn three crucial minutes.

There was every reason for the Eagles to lose this game.

They lacked cornerback Darius Slay, who was concussed. They lacked receiver DeVonta Smith, still hamstrung. They lacked Graham, who's done for the year. They lost big-play safety Reed Blankenship to a concussion late in the third quarter, and lost tight end Dallas Goedert to a knee injury in the fourth.

But they didn't lose the game. They won. Emphatically.

"We're a resilient football team. A determined team," Sirianni said. "This was a good win for us. This is a good football team we just played, with a lot of good players."

He understands how much this game means in the bigger picture.

The Eagles won in Brazil against the Packers, they beat the Commanders at home, and they demolished Dallas in Texas, but this was the sort of signature win that lends credibility. After collapsing last season and then starting this season 2-2, they need every ounce of credibility they can earn. On Sunday evening in Baltimore, they earned Super Bowl credibility. ∎

Tight end Dallas Goedert prepares to spike the football after catching a second-quarter touchdown pass. (Monica Herndon / Staff Photographer)

'He Would Just be Our Friend'

He used to be their babysitter.
Now, Saquon Barkley eyes the NFL record books

By Alex Coffey | Dec. 5, 2024

When Maisey Hartman arrived at St. Joseph's as a freshman last year, she decided to join a community service program. The teenager wasn't from Philadelphia and wanted to meet new people while giving back to the area.

On her first day, she walked into a room full of students. An upperclassman asked everyone to share a fun fact. Hartman began to worry. Nothing immediately came to mind.

But then, the perfect detail suddenly emerged.

"Saquon Barkley was my babysitter," Hartman said.

The students looked back at her with blank stares.

"What did you just say?" one of them asked.

"Saquon Barkley was my babysitter," she responded. "That's probably the only thing I can think of."

Hartman's classmates were astounded by her nonchalance. She didn't talk about the potential Hall of Famer in exalting terms. She didn't linger on the 1,312 yards he'd rushed for in 2022, his two Pro Bowl appearances, or the New York Giants franchise records he'd set.

She talked about him like she knew him — because she did.

Hartman, 19, grew up in Whitehall, Pa. Barkley lived in Coplay, which is about two miles away. She met him through her father, Bob Hartman, who is the longtime athletic director at Whitehall High School, which Barkley attended from 2011 to 2015.

They quickly became close. Bob Hartman saw a maturity in Barkley that was well beyond his years. For a player as gifted he was — Barkley amassed 3,646 rushing yards and 63 touchdowns at Whitehall — he didn't act as if he had all the answers. When Hartman called the running back into his office, he often would say, "What did I do wrong?"

The answer usually was nothing. But Hartman liked that Barkley was humble enough to ask.

"He was a very inquisitive kid," Hartman said. "More so than a normal high schooler."

Their conversations weren't always about football. Barkley would talk about his grades, the recruiting process, and life in general. It became clear to Hartman that he could trust him. So, in 2014, when he and his wife needed a backup babysitter, they asked a kid who one day would make NFL defenders look foolish.

Barkley said yes.

"I knew he could use the extra money, and my

Saquon Barkley smiles on the sideline after his fourth-quarter touchdown against the Los Angeles Rams on Nov. 24, 2024. (David Maialetti / Staff Photographer)

kids liked Saquon," Hartman said. "They looked up to him, and I knew they wouldn't get out of line. He was responsible. So it was sort of an easy decision."

From then on, Barkley began to fill in when the Hartmans' regular babysitter was unavailable. He babysat for Maisey and her older brother, Zack, about six times. They were young — Zack was in sixth grade and Maisey was in fourth — but they still have vivid memories from that era.

For Zack, who is 22 years old and a senior at Elon University, one memory stands out among the rest.

"I beat him in *Madden* [NFL]," he said. "I think the score was 31-28, or something like that. I remember he was the Browns, because Johnny Manziel had just gotten drafted. It was a close game, so it probably got intense. I can't imagine he was too happy about losing to a 12-year-old. But it was fun."

Zack made sure his family never forgot it. One time, he and his father were watching a Penn State game from home when they witnessed Barkley hurdle a player en route to a touchdown. The middle schooler was not impressed.

"I was like, 'Zack, did you see what Saquon just did?'" Bob Hartman said. "Zack goes, 'So what, Dad? I beat him in *Madden.*' That was always his trump card on Say: That he beat him in *Madden.*"

Maisey was shy growing up and didn't have much interest in football. But she liked that Barkley would talk to her while he played video games with her brother. Or he'd find other activities for them to do — like playing Jenga or Scrabble or watching a movie. It made her feel included.

"He was so nice and funny," Maisey said. "He made sure I didn't feel left out. He was really chill. He didn't really say, 'Make sure your teeth are brushed and you're in bed at this specific time.' He just made sure we were doing the right things.

"He wouldn't just watch us. He would actually hang out with us. Sometimes babysitters can be super strict — you have to do this at a certain time, you have to do this. He would just be our friend."

Barkley continued to be their friend. After he graduated from Whitehall in 2015, he stayed in touch with the Hartman family. He'd invite them to Penn State games and give them passes to see the locker room and the athletic facilities.

When he was a college freshman, he returned home one night for a high school football game. Students began to swarm him for autographs, but Maisey didn't want to be a bother. So she quietly stood to the side.

Barkley noticed.

"Hey, Maisey," he shouted with a grin. "You don't have time to say hi to your babysitter?"

She ran over and gave him a big hug. They took a photo together on the field. A few years later, Barkley returned to Whitehall to see Bob and his friend, soccer player Kayla Cunningham, get inducted into the school's hall of fame.

"We hadn't seen him in a while," Maisey said. "But he was like, 'How are you guys doing? Are you doing good in school?' He was just making sure we were OK. And that was really kind of him.

"It's been great to see him because I get worried … not that I had a huge impact on his life, but maybe that he would forget about me. Whenever I tell people I know Saquon, they say, 'Maisey, you really think he remembers you?' And I used to say, 'I don't know.' But he definitely remembers."

Things got a little more complicated when Barkley signed a three-year deal with the Eagles in March. Maisey, who is an Eagles fan, was thrilled. Her brother and her father — who are Dallas Cowboys fans — felt conflicted.

"I was hoping he'd go to the Dolphins or something," Zack said. "Now, I have to root for him, but against the Eagles. That's the hard part about it. But he earned a lot of money, and all his hard work has paid off. And he deserves that more than anyone."

Added Bob: "I can watch the games and compartmentalize. I want him to be successful. I want him to do great things. And that obviously

After six seasons with the New York Giants, Lehigh Valley native Saquon Barkley exceeded all expectations as a member of the Eagles. (David Maialetti / Staff Photographer)

comes with the Eagles' success.

"When he signed, I was like, 'Hey, listen, I'm so proud of you. Wish you the best. You deserve everything you get, but don't ever expect me to wear a green jersey.' And he just laughed."

The Hartmans try to go to a few of Barkley's NFL games every year. They don't always tell him when they're there. Bob tries to respect the running back's space. But regardless, they're always paying attention to what he's doing. And this year, they're paying extra close attention.

Barkley is on the precipice of history. He has rushed for 1,499 yards through 12 games this year. He is on pace to break the NFL's single-season rushing record of 2,105 set by Eric Dickerson of the Los Angeles Rams in 1984.

But that's not what Bob is proudest of.

"Obviously, the things he does on the field are amazing," Hartman said. "And I get these phone calls every time he does something crazy. But I'm just as proud of him as a father. He loves his two kids and treats them right. It's not an easy job. But I've seen him do it very, very well. And that's as good as any 255-yard game he has." ■

The Grind Doesn't Stop

With support from team leadership, Nick Sirianni has changed the way the Eagles practice

By EJ Smith

Toward the end of a victorious postgame speech earlier this season, Nick Sirianni answered a passing question so nonchalantly players weren't sure whether to believe him. *I'll see you Monday.*

In Sirianni's locker rooms and others across the NFL, terms like "victory Monday" and "walk-through Wednesday" quickly become phrases understood by all. Wins, especially late in the season, often earn players the next two days off, and padded practices early in the year typically give way to lighter walk-throughs to keep players healthy toward the end of the regular season.

So when Sirianni told the group a couple months ago that there wouldn't be any more victory Mondays this year, they almost didn't buy it. It had come out of nowhere for some. Maybe it was a ploy to motivate the group? Maybe they misheard him?

"He kind of sprung it on us," Eagles linebacker Nakobe Dean said. "He was like, 'Yeah, and we won't have any victory Mondays. We're working on Monday for the rest of the year.' I think it was Week 7 or Week 8. And we were like, 'Oh, OK. Maybe he's just kind of saying it for right now?' But, no, that's how it's been, and we've embraced it."

The change to the start of the week is one of a handful of adjustments Sirianni and his coaching staff have made this year in an effort to better prepare for the season's final stretch. It's a stretch the Eagles struggled with last year; they lost six of their final seven regular-season games, which sparked an offseason of conversations about how to address the sharp regression, conversations that included the team's leadership council more than in past offseasons.

Sirianni's added emphasis on Mondays was one of the by-products, something he said was reinforced by a request from quarterback Jalen Hurts, among others.

"I was thinking about it. [It was] one of the things I ruminated on over some of the things that happened last year and why I felt like some things happened," Sirianni told The Inquirer. "Even though we had a big win, we're going to come in here, and we're going to get better from this tape. ... And that was from some of the players, too. I talked to Jalen about it. Jalen was like, 'Hey, we need to put this game — we have to learn from the game.' I think we all came up with the same theory."

The approach to practice has changed as well. It was foreshadowed by a training camp

Linebacker Nakobe Dean says that Eagles players have embraced head coach Nick Sirianni's more intensive approach to team practices in 2024. (Monica Herndon / Staff Photographer)

that Sirianni warned would be more difficult than summers before and has now materialized into padded practices later into the season with an added emphasis on physicality.

Eagles left tackle Jordan Mailata said players may have been skeptical at first, but casting away some of the complacency that set in last season has been the result of Sirianni shaking things up.

"We had gotten comfortable," Mailata said. "We had gotten comfortable off the routine. Nick would always give us the victory Mondays, the walk-through on Wednesdays. But that's a long time off. That's three days off. And for guys that don't play in the game, that's five days off. That's a long time."

Dean added: "The first two years, if you think about it, we were almost [to] walk-through Wednesdays by Week 6 or Week 7. And we were off damn near every Monday that we won. So it's definitely been different, but it's been good. It's worked."

'Actually tackling a person'

Nearly every Wednesday since the Eagles' early-season bye week, safeties coach Joe Kasper stands about a yard in front of a mattress-sized pad, holding a step-over bag and bracing as Eagles defenders take turns running into him in quick succession.

It's a drill that looks worse than it actually is for the young coach, who generously measures in around 6 feet tall and less than 200 pounds.

If the players do it right, Kasper said, nobody gets hurt.

"I have an idea of how I want to fall," Kasper told The Inquirer. "I'm anticipating getting hit. I know how I want to fall; I know how to land on the pad so that I don't get dinged. And, honestly, one of the best parts about it, if it's not a proper tackle, I can feel like kind of firsthand. I know that's like, 'Well, man, that sounds kind of rough.' But truth be told, that's an effective way

to get a solution. I can feel if a player is too high. I can feel if a player isn't wrapping my hamstrings properly."

Kasper spent two years as a defensive quality control coach for the Eagles for the 2021 and 2022 seasons and rejoined the coaching staff as a safeties coach last offseason after one year with the same title for the Miami Dolphins. He ran a similar version of the drill in Miami and brought it to Sirianni because of an insistence that the players get more value "actually tackling a person" during practices.

Sirianni had a few tweaks, including adding a second assistant coach to emulate a blocker at the start of the drill, but eventually signed off.

After the team had 15 missed tackles, by defensive coordinator Vic Fangio's estimation against the Tampa Bay Buccaneers in Week 4, they came back from the bye two weeks later doing the drill, which was introduced in training camp.

Since then, Kasper's taken his share of hits with the team doing the drill nearly every week. Fortunately for him, the team's tackling has improved significantly since the early-season struggles, which means fewer times he's grimacing on the mat.

"Not as much as you'd think," Kasper said when asked how much punishment he's taking in recent weeks. "Really, to be honest with you, because we've been fortunate that we've been a good tackling team this year and we've done [the drill] the right way."

According to Pro Football Focus, the Eagles have missed 10 or more tackles just once since the bye week. The lone time surpassing double digits came last Sunday against the Baltimore Ravens' backfield duo of Lamar Jackson and Derrick Henry, but the defense even made key tackles in that game. One of those key tackles, made by Cooper DeJean on Henry in the fourth quarter of the 24-19 win, Sirianni said resembled the work the defense does in practice with one key distinction.

"To be able to tackle a body, and we don't go to the ground, so this is an opportunity to do so," Sirianni said. "It really looked like Coop's tackle — now Derrick Henry is a heck of a lot bigger than Joe Kasper — but it's a credit to our assistant coaches for putting them in situations."

One season removed from fielding one of the worst defenses in the NFL, the Eagles now rank in the top five of several defensive categories this season with a physicality that traces back to uptick in practice sessions Fangio has advocated for since joining the team this offseason.

While the sentiment the veteran coach said earlier this week may have been the most playful version, Fangio has consistently harped on the importance of practice reps for a defense with an average age of 24.4 years old last Sunday.

"The more you practice, the more you play, you get better, in spite of what Allen Iverson ever said," Fangio said jokingly on Tuesday.

'It takes what it takes'

Among players on the Eagles roster, Oren Burks may have the easiest adjustment to the increased amount of late-season padded practices the Eagles have held.

Coming from the San Francisco 49ers, Burks said his previous experience left him already accustomed to putting the pads on even in the weeks leading up to the playoffs for continuity entering the biggest games of the season.

"I think it was just establishing what the mindset of this year is going to be," Burks said. "'It takes what it takes.' We're not looking for an easy way out. We're sticking to our process, and that's been showing up every week the last couple weeks. For us to play the ball we know we're capable of, that takes getting in the film room, getting on the same page, and that physicality that we talk about

in putting the pads on. That's showing up."

Burks' comparison to the Niners' practice regimen tracks somewhat with comments made by Javon Hargrave last year. Hargrave, a defensive tackle who spent 2020 to 2022 with the Eagles before signing with the Niners in free agency, said the Eagles' practice habits were "more relaxed" compared to his new team's.

Although Hargrave's comments caught the ire of his former teammates, including former Eagles defensive tackle Fletcher Cox, there's an inkling of truth there. The Eagles' emphasis on load management under Sirianni has cut both ways in the last few years and is still prevalent in areas this season. The team had all 22 of its Week 1 starters healthy for Super Bowl LVII two years ago with a more lenient approach to Wednesday practices, and several players said Sirianni still finds ways to balance the tougher Wednesday practices with lighter sessions at other points of the week.

"I think Nick really stood back and said, 'We didn't work enough at all last year,'" Mailata said. "So that's been the emphasis."

With a younger team and a coordinator in Fangio who has consistently pushed for more reps for his youthful defense, this may be the first time the Eagles use all of the padded practices the NFL's collective bargaining agreement allows for under Sirianni. According to overthecap.com, the CBA permits teams to hold 14 padded sessions during the regular season with limitations on how many can be used during the final handful of weeks.

Eagles right tackle Lane Johnson said Sirianni came to the him and the team's leadership earlier this year with the plan to use them all and to space them out more toward the back half of the season.

"You only have a certain amount, but we saved some for this time of the year," Johnson said. "Because it is weird when you go from walk-throughs all week and not having hardly any full-speed padded [reps], it can catch you off guard. But I think we've done a good job with how we've done things this year."

Sirianni added: "We've had a couple more, that's no doubt. ... I don't want to correlate to this because you still do it, but if you're a basketball player and you play once a week, it would be crazy if we didn't shoot during the week."

Aside from tackling drills, the team also has done one-on-one pass-rushing drills between offensive and defensive linemen during the parts of practice closed to the media, something most teams typically discard by this point in the season. Wednesdays generally are focused on the offensive and defensive line and the run game to take advantage of the time in pads.

"A lot of teams don't do that," Johnson said. "When you do walk-throughs all the time throughout the week and you only have full speed against pads in the game, it can kind of catch you off guard. Trying to get that in on a Wednesday can do a lot of good for you."

While the current approach seemingly has yielded results, it's important to note Sirianni's previous prioritization of preserving players with lighter workloads late in the year was also a major factor in the team's relatively healthy finishes each of the last two years. The new one may invite more injury risk. Eagles defensive tackle Jalen Carter suffered a shoulder injury in practice earlier this season but didn't miss any game time as a result. Linebacker Ben VanSumeren suffered a season-ending knee injury in practice last week, but that was during the final practice session of the week and not in pads.

The team also has turned to resting a handful of veterans, including Johnson, Saquon Barkley, edge rusher Josh Sweat, and Carter for part of Wednesday sessions to preserve the group with the heaviest workloads during games.

"If you look at '22 and how healthy we were, I think that's something that you could very much look upon and be like, 'This is the way to do it,'" Sirianni said. "Well, there are different factors with the 2022 team than there are with the 2024 team. The experience, things like that. So there are things that you need to continue to get better at."

And while there may not be a Monday off in the coming weeks, Sirianni hasn't ruled out the potential for it to return eventually.

Until then, Sirianni is hanging onto the response — genuine or otherwise — he got from the players in M&T Bank Stadium last Sunday when he told them Monday once again would be a workday, as it has for the last couple months.

"The guys were cheering. I don't know if they were cheering sarcastically or not," Sirianni said. "I was like, 'Hey, we're working tomorrow,' and they were like, 'Yeah! We're working.'" ∎

Linemen like Lane Johnson supported Nick Sirianni's new training program that saw more padded practices during the week balanced with strategic rest. (Monica Herndon / Staff Photographer)

DEC. 8, 2024
LINCOLN FINANCIAL FIELD
EAGLES 22, PANTHERS 16

Winning Ugly

Saquon Barkley makes history as the Eagles grind out ninth straight win

By Olivia Reiner

When the Carolina Panthers attempted a comeback late in the fourth quarter on Sunday afternoon, Darius Slay called game.

In his return from a concussion that sidelined him last week against the Baltimore Ravens, the 33-year-old outside cornerback broke up a pass from quarterback Bryce Young intended for wide receiver Adam Thielen on fourth-and-9 deep in Eagles territory with 29 seconds left, sealing a 22-16 home victory for the Eagles. The play followed a drop from wide receiver Xavier Legette short of the goal line on a deep ball from Young that could have helped flip the score in Carolina's favor.

Slay's big play served as one of the highlights from a shaky overall performance from the Eagles defense, which gave up more than 300 net yards of offense for just the fifth time this season.

Slow to start

True to form, the Eagles offense came out sluggish to start the game. For the 10th contest this season, Jalen Hurts and the rest of the unit failed to put up points in the first quarter. Saquon Barkley got going early in the second quarter on their third possession (five carries for 37 yards) to set the Eagles up for a Tush Push touchdown and put them up, 7-3.

Still, the passing game remained listless, as Hurts went 4-for-9 for 42 yards through four possessions. A.J. Brown wasn't targeted on any of those drives.

C.J. Gardner-Johnson provided the Eagles the spark they needed to get back into a rhythm. With two minutes remaining in the first half, the 26-year-old safety picked off Young on a third-and-3 play from the Carolina 36-yard line on a pass intended for Thielen, bringing the Eagles offense back on the field at the Panthers' 44.

Hurts got back into a brief groove in the passing game and got the ball back in the hands of his top receiver. Brown snared his first target and reception of the game with 1 minute, 26 seconds left in the first half. Hurts completed all five of his passes on the drive, capped by a 4-yard touchdown pass to DeVonta Smith, who returned after missing two games with a hamstring injury.

Grant Calcaterra got in on the action, too, making his first career touchdown reception on a 4-yard pass early in the fourth quarter to pull the Eagles ahead, 20-16. After a Carolina penalty, Barkley ran in a two-point conversion to make it 22-16.

The offense was still inconsistent at times, as Hurts took four sacks and threw for only 108 yards. Brown finished the game with four receptions on four targets for 43 yards, his second-lowest total of the season.

When asked what is holding the Eagles' passing game back, Hurts succinctly pointed to a "lack of synchronization." Hurts was also asked whether he thinks the Eagles' conversation about getting on the same page should be happening in Week 14, to which he responded, "No."

Meanwhile, Jake Elliott was hard to trust beyond the 50-yard line, as he missed a 52-yard field-goal attempt in the third quarter. The Eagles opted to punt on fourth-and-9 instead of attempt another long field goal to precede the final Panthers possession, a decision that Nick Sirianni chalked up to the wind blowing in the opposite direction of the drive. Still, the running game and the defense's big stand in the final seconds were enough to survive the Panthers' attempted comeback.

Barkley sets franchise record

Going into Sunday's game, Barkley had the opportunity to break the single-season franchise rushing record, set by LeSean McCoy in 2013. The 27-year-old running back needed just 109 yards to best McCoy's total of 1,607 in 16 games.

Barkley made it happen in 13, surpassing McCoy with a 9-yard carry more than halfway through the fourth quarter to bring his total on the day to 116 yards. He finished the game with 124 yards on 20 carries, marking his ninth game of the season with 100-plus rushing yards, also a franchise record.

The star running back knew that he could break the record going into Sunday's game, but he didn't know in the moment of his 9-yard run that he had eclipsed the previous high.

"I think it's pretty cool," Barkley said. "The most important thing was getting a win, and we got a win. But being a fan of Shady growing up and seeing the spectacular things he was able to do with the ball in his hands. And just to be able to have my name mentioned with him definitely means a lot. But a lot of credit to the guys up front. They made my job a lot easier."

His most impressive play of the day came early in the third quarter when he ripped off an 18-yard run to move the offense to midfield. Jordan Mailata's block on safety Xavier Woods at the second level of the Panthers defense helped spring Barkley as the running back took off to the left outside the numbers. However, the Eagles were unable to capitalize on the play, as Elliott missed the 52-yard field-goal attempt. ∎

DEC. 15, 2024
LINCOLN FINANCIAL FIELD
EAGLES 27, STEELERS 13

On the Same Page

A.J. Brown and the Eagles' passing game do the talking after
a week of 'uncomfortable conversations'

By EJ Smith

A.J. Brown spotted the light aircraft circling over Lincoln Financial Field on his ride over to the stadium. Attached to the plane was a banner that read in all caps, "ENOUGH FAKE NEWS! PHILLY STANDS WITH 1 & 11."

"That was cool," Brown said with a chuckle. "That was cool."

A few hours later, Nos. 1 (Jalen Hurts) and 11 (Brown), hooked up for the Eagles' first touchdown in their eventual 27-13 victory over the Pittsburgh Steelers, and after the receiver scored he beelined to his quarterback and the pair celebrated like Kid 'n Play in *House Party*.

"That was our moment," Brown said, "to tell everybody to shut up."

There were other moments more important than the dance — and plenty of them — to show that Brown and Hurts were simpatico. But the former's role in drawing attention to what ailed the passing offense a week ago — and caused Brandon Graham to initially declare the tandem no longer friends — shouldn't go unnoticed.

Graham walked back his comments, but he gave speculators the ammunition they needed to question Brown and Hurts' relationship. But Brown wasn't apologizing for cracking a few eggs if it meant fixing the Eagles' air attack.

On a day in which Hurts had his best passing performance of the season, and the Eagles' top two receivers caught a combined 19 passes for 219 yards and two touchdowns, Brown agreed that his public airing helped lead to Sunday's result.

"Absolutely," he said. "I said it for a reason. I didn't have ill intentions behind it. It wasn't for me to get the ball. It was just for us to all get on the same page and put our best foot forward. We know what we're capable of, and last week wasn't our standard.

"It's just crazy, though, because everybody in the locker room said the same thing, and I kind of got crucified for it. But it was cool."

DeVonta Smith, Jordan Mailata, and Hurts also weren't satisfied with last week's passing performance in a lackluster win over the Carolina Panthers. But the frustration from Brown had been

Following tense conversations about the state of the Eagles' passing game, Jalen Hurts, A.J. Brown, and the receiving corps combined for 19 catches and 219 yards against the Steelers. (Yong Kim / Staff Photographer)

building for weeks as the Eagles kept winning behind the strength of Saquon Barkley and the running game.

Sure, Brown wants the ball and wants to have an impact. Smith has the same confidence in his ability to affect the outcome. But they knew there would come a time when Hurts would have to drop back more than hand off and that time, fittingly, came against one of the NFL's better defenses in Pittsburgh.

The Steelers devoted additional defenders in stopping Barkley. But the Eagles knew that was likely to happen coming in, and they knew Hurts would have opportunities to take advantage of coverages that could be predictable.

"We're going to focus on what we need to do, not what everybody else thinks we need to do," said Eagles coach Nick Sirianni. "Our focus and our main thing for each and every week is how do we win this football game? Today we had to pass for 290 yards, and that was just a great job by our guys."

It was clear from the get-go, though, that Sirianni and offensive coordinator Kellen Moore were going to try to rebuild Hurts' confidence in his arm. On the very first play, the Eagles opened with an empty backfield and the quarterback hit tight end Grant Calcaterra on a seam route for 22 yards.

Three of the next four plays went to Brown or Smith. The offense stalled and settled for a field goal. Moore went heavy on the ground on the next series, but that's when it became clear that the Steelers often had an extra man in the box.

The Eagles were forced to punt for Braden Mann's lone boot of the game. And for the next 2½ quarters, Hurts and his receivers carved up the Pittsburgh back seven. They didn't do so on downfield throws, however. Calcaterra's catch was Hurts' longest in terms of air yards.

It was short-to-intermediate routes that exposed the Steelers — early in the game on downs vs. man coverage and later on downs vs. zone. Brown pulled in throws on slants and back shoulders near the sideline, while Smith did much of his work on crossing routes and grabs over the middle.

All told, the receivers were targeted 23 times — the most since over a year ago vs. the Cowboys. And their combined 19 catches — Brown had eight for 110 yards and Smith 11 for 109 yards — were the most they've had in three years together.

Hurts, overall, completed 25 of 32 passes for 290 yards.

"So that's what you all wanted to see, huh?" Hurts said as he sat down at the podium before any questions were asked at his postgame news conference.

He could have posed the question to Brown, as well. But, yes, it answered some of the doubts that had crept in — really, since the end of last season — about Hurts' ability to see the field and get the ball out in rhythm.

He wasn't perfect. He had an early fumble on a scramble and took three sacks over a span of four plays before the half. But this was Hurts executing the offense and taking what a defense was giving him. The Eagles had multiple third-down conversions after he checked the ball down.

"He played a great game," Brown said of Hurts. "He took what they gave him, and the wideouts and tight ends and everybody was just good with yards after the catch. And that's needed."

Hurts confirmed that he had broken his left ring finger last week and said it had affected his performance. He wore a glove on his non-throwing hand with tape and a splint on his finger. It was unclear when the injury occurred or if it played a role in his inefficiency against Carolina.

But Hurts' struggles had predated the injury. The Eagles have run more than most offenses since he became the starter in 2021. But the imbalance this season was at an all-time high and it was fair to wonder if the passing game had become atrophied as a result.

Sirianni said that notion was overplayed.

"I think it kind of gets a little bit blown out of proportion," Sirianni said. "Jalen's quarterback rating has been over 100 most of the games. I don't know what he was today [125.3], but most of the games he's been over 100. We're averaging 8.5-plus in the pass game."

And yet, Brown and Smith said the Eagles had "repetitive" meetings last week to clean up details and that there were "uncomfortable conversations" between the receivers and Hurts about being on the same page and in sync in their communication.

"Very uncomfortable," Brown said. "First of all, I didn't call anybody out, but behind closed doors, yeah, we talk about that, we call each other out. And that's very uncomfortable because you don't want to feel like you're getting attacked.

"But we're not in this for feelings. We're trying to get on the same page. We trying to win, most importantly."

It was one of the stranger weeks in recent Eagles history, even if the team insisted that speculation about potential turmoil was much ado about nothing. Clearly, there was something. But how much often depends on who's doing the telling.

"For me, it's like, I'm gonna skip the Real Housewives of [expletive] Philadelphia channel. I'm gonna go to something else," Eagles tackle Lane Johnson said Sunday after being absent from open locker room last week. "But the way I see it, man, brothers fight sometimes. We put a lot into this. Emotions run high."

He added: "You have a lot of talented guys. I think coming together tonight showing, especially throwing the ball, what we're able to do, I think that maybe it's done some healing. Hopefully, it did."

The Eagles' victory gave them a franchise-best 10th straight, and at 12-2 they are just a tiebreaker behind the also 12-2 Lions.

Brown has only one objective. He got to the Super Bowl two years ago, along with Hurts and Smith, and the Eagles nearly won it behind the explosiveness of their passing game. They know what it will take to get back there and win.

"We know the end goal is, especially me, DeVonta and Jalen," Brown said. "We've been here, and like I said in the past, we trying to get to the end, and we trying to finish. It's good we won 10 [straight] games, but we're not satisfied with that.

"Honestly, in our mind, we haven't done nothing."

They've done more than nothing, but there's something about setting the bar at its highest rung. ∎

DEC. 22, 2024

LANDOVER, MD.

COMMANDERS 36, EAGLES 33

Coming Up Short

Jalen Hurts out with concussion as Eagles fail to clinch NFC East

By Jeff Neiburg

DeVonta Smith took about six steps toward Noah Igbinoghene, and the Washington cornerback was backpedaling as Smith cut to his right and looked back at Kenny Pickett. Smith was open, wide-open, as Pickett threw the ball his way.

It was third-and-5 from Washington's 22-yard line, the Eagles were ahead by two, and the two-minute warning was nearing. Washington had just used its penultimate timeout. It was the type of play every receiver wants to make. Smith later said he was calling for the ball.

"When they put it in my hand I got to make the g— play," he said.

He didn't. The dropped pass, a rarity for the sure-handed Smith, gave the Commanders life in their eventual 36-33 victory Sunday at Northwest Stadium.

"I just dropped the ball," Smith said. "I ain't going to beat myself up over it. That's life, part of the game. I made all the tough catches today, and then the easiest one I had I dropped. It is what it is. Charge it to the game. Ain't nobody else's fault but mine."

Smith took the blame for the Eagles' loss, but it was hardly all on him. The Eagles lost for a variety of reasons. Pickett was playing because Jalen Hurts went down with a concussion five minutes into the

game. The Eagles gave up more than 23 points for the first time since September. They were undisciplined. They were, as Nick Sirianni said, "sloppy."

But despite an imperfect game from Pickett, and a rushing attack that, save for Saquon Barkley's 68-yard scoring scamper, was bottled up, the offense had a chance to seal the game for the Eagles and clinch a division title. If Smith caught the ball, the Eagles would've been on the right side of the two-minute warning, first-and-goal from inside the 10-yard line, and with a chance to put the game away with a touchdown. At the very least, they could have taken enough time off the clock to make a last-second drive for Jayden Daniels and the Commanders next to impossible.

"We wouldn't be in the position in that game without him to begin with," Pickett said. "He's an unbelievable player. He knows that we're going to throw him the football, [and] A.J. [Brown too], no matter what."

He meant that quite literally. The star Eagles receivers accounted for 23 of the 25 passing targets on the day.

Pickett came onto the field after Hurts left the game after a designed quarterback run for 13 yards ended with his head appearing to hit the turf. Hurts went to the medical tent and then jogged to the locker room, never returning to the sideline. Pickett finished that drive efficiently and connected with Brown on a 4-yard touchdown pass.

Pickett was at times erratic. He overthrew Brown and Smith on some passes and threw behind them on others. With Hurts out of the game, the Commanders dared the Eagles to beat them with Pickett's arm. They stacked the box and took Barkley out of the game. Take Barkley's 68-yard touchdown run off his stat line, and he rushed 28 times for 82 yards. That's fewer than 3 yards per carry.

"A lot of our stuff is built on Jalen being able to run the ball," Barkley said. "It's kind of hard to run the same stuff.

"They did a really good job of adjusting. Usually, we're the team that adjusts better in the second half and we've shown that throughout the whole season. We, as a whole, didn't do enough. When that happens, you tend to lose football games."

Still, it was winnable. Even after Pickett threw an interception that set Washington up with a short field. Even after the playbook had to change. Even after Barkley dropped a pass on a wheel route one drive before Smith's drop.

The Eagles offense spent an entire afternoon adjusting on the fly, and it nearly worked.

"They're two different players," Brown said. "Kenny was just trying to get situated and get his feet up under him. He hasn't played all year. He did at times and sometimes he got rattled. There was a lot going on. They were pressuring him a lot, changing the looks up. I feel like he did well to handle everything."

Pickett finished 14-for-24 for 143 yards. Hurts' status is not yet known. Pickett, who will

have further testing done Monday on a rib injury, said he always prepares like he's the starter and will continue to do that at the beginning of this week while more is learned about Hurts. That preparation, though, goes only so far.

"It's tough," Pickett said about coming in cold. "You don't get any physical snaps. I just try to do the best I can, mentally locked into the game plan, understanding the checks and really how these guys run routes because I don't get a chance to throw it to them."

Asked if Sunday was a valuable experience, Pickett said it was difficult to frame it that way.

"I'm honestly just sitting here just [ticked] off, man," he said. "I wanted to win that one bad, point blank."

He nearly did.

"He played good," Smith said of Pickett. "I think he settled in well. I think he made the right reads. ... It's just unfortunate I didn't make the last play." ∎

DEC. 29, 2024
LINCOLN FINANCIAL FIELD
EAGLES 41, COWBOYS 7

His Finest Hour

Nick Sirianni leads the depleted Eagles to an NFC East title

By Marcus Hayes

The Eagles had every excuse to lose.

They were playing their archrivals, the Cowboys, for the second time this season. The Cowboys were out of playoff contention, but they had won four of five games, including a win at Washington, the site of the Eagles' latest disaster, and they were playing with abandon, visiting a team haunted by collapses both distant and recent.

The week before, the Birds blew a 14-point lead at Washington, where they lost quarterback Jalen Hurts to a concussion that lingered through Sunday, Hurts' first missed game of the season. Worse, the Eagles' top-ranked defense had lost its composure, and the game, at Washington. Finally, on Sunday, not only was the offense's quarterback absent, so was the defense's quarterback: Middle linebacker Nakobe Dean missed Sunday's game due to an abdominal strain.

They had every excuse to lose. They didn't lose. Nick Sirianni wouldn't have it.

Several players said afterward that Sirianni this past week reiterated this axiom:

"You can't be great without the greatness of others."

It's that sort of saying that has been the hallmark of Sirianni's astounding success. He's 47-20 in the regular season, has the best winning percentage among active coaches, and secured a fourth straight playoff appearance Sunday.

From Monday to Sunday, no one in the Eagles Nation was greater than Sirianni.

In a 13-win campaign that saw the Birds clinch the NFC East with a week left, it was, in many ways, Sirianni's finest hour of the season.

"Amazing," said tackle Jordan Mailata. "In many ways, I think that was our best complementary football of the season."

It was a ticklish spot for Sirianni, who's had a hell of a season. He'd been questioned after a 2-2 start, which followed a 1-5 collapse in 2023 and a blowout loss in the playoffs. He'd been pilloried after Game 5, when he taunted Eagles fans after a home win. Game 5 was the start of a franchise-record 10-game winning streak, in which a more composed, mature Sirianni guided the team to blowout wins in Cincinnati and Dallas as well as decisive victories over the Commanders, Rams, Ravens, and Steelers. A pass-first coach, Sirianni had leaned on Saquon Barkley, who, in the fourth quarter, became the ninth player to eclipse 2,000 rushing yards in a season; at

Wide receiver DeVonta Smith celebrates after catching a 22-yard touchdown pass during the second quarter. (Monica Herndon / Staff Photographer)

2,005, he passed O.J. Simpson's best season, in 1973 with the Bills, but remains 100 yards behind Eric Dickerson's 1984 record, set with the Rams.

Sirianni's next big decision: Will he let Barkley play in a probably meaningless finale against the Giants next week?

"We'll see."

"If it's in God's plan," Barkley said, "then it is. I didn't come here just to rush for 2,000 or break a record. It's up to Nick."

It's a nice decision to have to make, especially considering the more pressing problems he dealt with this past week and the weight carried by Sunday's game against the Cowboys.

Last week's messy loss, combined with Hurts' injury, added to a postgame dustup with former Eagles tight end Zach Ertz, put the focus on Sirianni again. He'd been a Coach of the Year candidate for a month. He'd seemingly earned a contract extension; his expires after next season.

But a loss to the Cowboys and a win by the Commanders would have put the division title in jeopardy, and, perhaps, Sirianni's future.

Sirianni proved equal to the task.

"We had a great atmosphere, you know?" cornerback Quinyon Mitchell said. "Coach came in and said, 'We have to look ourselves in the mirror. Clean up some mistakes.' So, in practice, we honed in. This week was executed, mentally, really well."

Sirianni prepared backup quarterback Kenny Pickett, whose style of play is entirely opposite to that of Hurts.

He prepared third-string rookie Tanner McKee, who threw a 20-yard touchdown pass to A.J. Brown for a dagger late in the third quarter, then added a 25-yarder to DeVonta Smith in the fourth.

He controlled Jalen Carter, who led the league with four unnecessary roughness penalties, and C.J. Gardner-Johnson, who was ejected at Washington for two unsportsmanlike conduct fouls. Carter's disappearance and Gardner-Johnson's absence led to 22 fourth-quarter points in the Commanders' comeback win.

Carter was outstanding on Sunday.

Gardner-Johnson? Amazing. Two interceptions. A pick-six on the first Commanders' possession. With Hurts out of action, he even broke down the pregame huddle.

"He responded awesome," Sirianni said, and said it was a manifestation of Sirianni's "dog mentality" philosophy: "Learning from your mistakes, but putting them in the past, and being able to focus completely on where you're at right now. That won't only serve him well in football, it will serve him well in life."

It served Sirianni well on Sunday. Really, he was never better.

He featured Smith, knowing the Cowboys would sell out to stop Brown. Smith had six catches for 120 yards and two touchdowns. Brown had three catches for 36 yards and a score.

Nothing mattered more than preparing Pickett.

Pickett recognized a six-man blitz and hit Smith for a 22-yard touchdown and a 14-7 lead. He was part of four short-yardage Tush Pushes, three of which worked, the fourth for a touchdown as the first half expired with the Eagles leading, 24-7. He completed 10 of 15 passes for 143 yards and the touchdown before a hit from Micah Parsons aggravated a rib injury Pickett suffered at Washington and knocked him from the game.

"It's very much a college-team feel," Pickett said afterward. "Everyone cares about each other. That's incredibly special."

With Pickett hobbled and with McKee an unknown entity, Sirianni knew the Birds would have to ride Barkley. They did: They gave the ball to Barkley on six of the first seven plays of the third

Though his decision-making was widely questioned early in the 2024 season, Nick Sirianni, left, successfully managed the injury-addled Eagles to a win over the Cowboys that secured the NFC East title. (Monica Herndon / Staff Photographer)

quarter, and he gained 30 yards as the Eagles made four first downs, used almost seven minutes, and came away with a 26-yard field goal for a 20-point lead. Barkley finished with 167 yards, the fifth-highest rushing total of his career, the third-highest total of this season, and his 11th 100-yard rushing game this season. He did it on 31 rushes, which tied for the third-highest total of his career.

This was not the Cowboys team that began the season as a playoff favorite. It lacked quarterback Dak Prescott, defensive end DeMarcus Lawrence, receiver CeeDee Lamb, guard Zack Martin, and cornerback Trevon Diggs, five of Dallas' six best players, excepting Parsons. Also, Mike McCarthy remains their coach.

So no, the Cowboys weren't good. But, since Sirianni was hired in 2021, the Eagles have lost to plenty of teams that weren't good. Occasionally, Sirianni has been the problem.

On Sunday, he was the solution. ∎

JAN. 5, 2025
LINCOLN FINANCIAL FIELD
EAGLES 20, GIANTS 13

Answering the Call

The Eagles' wild-card matchup is set after capping 14-3 regular season

By Olivia Reiner

With the regular season in the books following a 20-13 victory over the New York Giants, the Eagles' wild-card matchup is set. The No. 2-seeded Eagles (14-3) will take on the No. 7-seeded Green Bay Packers (11-6) to kick off the postseason.

In the Packers' 24-22 loss to the Chicago Bears that solidified their seeding, quarterback Jordan Love went down with an elbow injury in the second quarter and did not return to action. Coach Matt LaFleur said after the game that Love was "good to go" back into the game, but that he was held out as a precaution. Receiver Christian Watson was carted off with a noncontact knee injury in the second and was later ruled out, casting uncertainty around his availability in the wild-card game.

The Eagles last faced the Packers in the season opener in São Paulo, Brazil, pulling off a 34-29 victory over the NFC North team. Saquon Barkley made a statement in his Eagles debut with three total touchdowns, two rushing and one receiving. That game was the only non-divisional loss for the 11-6 Packers, as they went on to lose all four of their games against the Minnesota Vikings

and the Detroit Lions and the Week 18 game against the Bears.

"Both teams are different from that day till now, no doubt," Eagles coach Nick Sirianni said of the Week 1 matchup. "You'll use that. You use everything. That's something that when we go play a team that we played the previous year, we'll use that, too. So that's from year to year. Of course, we'll use that. They'll use that. We understand that. It's a really good team. Really well-coached."

The Packers and the Eagles are no strangers in the postseason. The two franchises have met in the playoffs three times dating back to 1933. Most recently, the Packers defeated the Eagles in the 2010 wild-card round on their way to winning Super Bowl XLV. The Eagles have the 2-1 all-time edge in the postseason.

In a loaded NFC North, the Packers continued to build on last season's success, which ended in the divisional round of the playoffs. Love has been steady in his second year as the starter, tied for eighth in the league in passing touchdowns (25) going into Sunday's slate of games. Josh Jacobs, the 26-year-old running back the Packers added in free agency,

With quarterback Jalen Hurts still in concussion protocol, Eagles 2023 draft pick Tanner McKee made his first career NFL start against the Giants. (Yong Kim / Staff Photographer)

finished the season ranked third in the league in rushing yards behind Barkley and Baltimore Ravens tailback Derrick Henry.

Meanwhile, all eyes are on the health of Jalen Hurts going into the upcoming week of practice. The fourth-year starting quarterback sustained a concussion in Week 16 against the Washington Commanders and has not practiced since exiting that game. Sirianni confirmed after the game against the Giants that Hurts was present at the Eagles' walk-through on Saturday as he is "progressing" through the protocol.

McKee makes first start

Early in his first NFL start, McKee picked up where he left off last week when he saw his first regular-season action against the Dallas Cowboys. The 2023 sixth-rounder out of Stanford was poised and confident in the pocket for most of the afternoon, completing 27 passes on 41 attempts for 269 yards and two touchdowns.

The Eagles got out to a fast start on their opening possession thanks to the connection between McKee and tight end Dallas Goedert, who made his return to action after spending the last four weeks on injured reserve with a knee issue. On the first Eagles play of the day at their own 48-yard line after the defense forced a turnover on downs on the Giants' opening possession, McKee completed a 16-yard pass to Goedert on a play-action rollout. One play later, McKee found Goedert again on an out-breaking route for a gain of 17 yards to the red zone.

Goedert's efforts set up a play-action touchdown pass to rookie receiver Ainias Smith, the first of his NFL career, to put the Eagles up, 7-0. With most of the starters resting, McKee only had the luxury of Goedert in his receiving corps for the first two series. The 30-year-old tight end finished the day with four receptions for 55 yards.

Jahan Dotson, the team's third receiver behind A.J. Brown and DeVonta Smith, made his most

substantial impact in an Eagles uniform against the Giants. The 24-year-old receiver hauled in a season-high seven receptions for 94 yards, including a 19-yarder over the middle of the field late in the third quarter to land the Eagles deep in New York territory. That play led to E.J. Jenkins' 7-yard touchdown catch, marking the first of the tight end's career.

The Eagles had a few shaky moments on offense that contributed to their three punts on the afternoon. Behind a backup offensive line, McKee took a pair of sacks, one from Giants outside linebacker Kayvon Thibodeaux in the third quarter and another split between Thibodeaux and defensive lineman Elijah Garcia in the fourth. McKee nearly threw an interception late in the second quarter on a pass intended for Dotson with Giants cornerback Dru Phillips and safety Dane Belton nearby. Still, the 6-foot-6, 231-pound quarterback was satisfied with his overall performance in the win.

"I just felt like I showed that I have confidence in myself to go out and operate, run the offense," McKee said. "And, I feel like, for me, it just showed that my preparation has been working, and my preparation has helped me just get to how the offense was run today. And obviously, there's a ton of things that we can change; we're going to go back and watch film, and there's a lot of things that, different checks or progression, or something that I did wrong. So obviously, for me, it was a growing opportunity, which was great."

Giants' rally falls short

The Eagles defense, which featured backups and a couple of regular contributors such as Jordan Davis, prevented the Drew Lock-led Giants from generating explosive plays until the fourth quarter. On third-and-8 from the Eagles' 45, top Giants receiver Malik Nabers beat Eli Ricks off the line of scrimmage and hauled in a deep shot outside of the numbers from Lock. The rookie walked the tightrope down the right sideline to stay in bounds

Tight end E.J. Jenkins celebrates with Grant Calcaterra and teammates following a fourth-quarter touchdown, the first of Jenkins' NFL career. (Monica Herndon / Staff Photographer)

before somersaulting into the end zone.

His touchdown pulled the Giants within seven points, as the Eagles led, 17-10. But the defense held strong on the next Giants possession. Despite the Giants starting the drive at the Eagles' 38-yard line following a backed-up punt from the 15 and a 25-yard return from Ihmir Smith-Marsette, the defense limited them to a field goal.

The Eagles were up, 17-13, with 7 minutes, 21 seconds remaining in the game and they did not give up the ball until 47 seconds were left on the clock.

A 16-play, 36-yard, 6:34 drive that ended with a Jake Elliott field goal to put Philadelphia up, 20-13, ate up the clock and limited the Giants' likelihood of a comeback. Sydney Brown made the game-sealing interception with 24 seconds left.

"That's what we always go for," Brown said. "We always go for the ball, right? But it was a great effort all around. The linebackers playing their [butts] off. A lot of credit to them. A lot of credit to the D-linemen for making plays." ■

'Dark Times' Steel Saquon

Inside Saquon Barkley's workouts and the mentality that fuels him

By EJ Smith | Jan. 11, 2025

Saquon Barkley's phone buzzed in his locker stall with no one around to hear.

Just before the halftime whistle of the Eagles' penultimate regular-season game, the running back received a text message from longtime trainer Moe Gibson that he wouldn't see until hours later.

RELAX!!!

Gibson was watching Barkley attempt to make history from a powerless position, a few hours away and staring at the television screen. A decade spent on the grass with the star running back had formed a certain level of telepathy between the two, enough so that he could tell with each juke, cut, or burst upfield that Barkley executed that his proximity to greatness was front of mind.

Barkley wasn't the only one. Gibson had noticed the "extra chip" on the running back's shoulder in the months leading up to his first year with the Eagles and was watching the work that followed materialize with increasing anticipation.

So with just 268 yards between Barkley and the NFL's single-season rushing record entering the Week 17 game against the Dallas Cowboys, Gibson could feel that Barkley was pressing.

"It looked like he was trying to get 268 yards on every run," Gibson said, "instead of allowing it to just take what's there."

The Eagles are set to face the Green Bay Packers in Sunday's wild-card round largely because of Barkley's historic season. It was preceded by a rigorous offseason regimen tailored over the course of a seven-year career, one that featured Barkley pinging between longtime trainers, including Gibson and former Lehigh University receiver Troy Pelletier.

The focus was clear: longevity, endurance, and the desire to prove he was still among the best players in the NFL while embarking on the next chapter of his career.

"He had a fresh start and a fresh opportunity to rewrite a story," Pelletier said. "It gave him a lot of enthusiasm and a lot to look forward to this season. You could kind of see it in his commitment all offseason, just how hard he went in those workouts."

'Success is not an accident'

Sitting in the basement of the Whitehall High School field house a few weeks before training camp, Saquon Barkley seemed to know what would come next.

Saquon Barkley's MVP-worthy form in 2024 was backed by significant personal and financial investments in his training and health. (Yong Kim / Staff Photographer)

Perhaps not the specifics. Not the 2,005 rushing yards, the 345 carries, or the 378 total touches, all of which were the most in the league during the regular season. What he did know was it was time to dismiss the years-old debate about the erosive nature of his position.

Given the fruitless multiyear contract negotiations with the New York Giants and the apparent skepticism across the NFL about the viability of running backs with the workload Barkley has taken on during his career, it was understandable. A few months after signing a three-year contract with the Eagles worth $37.75 million, Barkley didn't mince words about those who loudly wondered how he'd hold up during the duration of that deal.

"There's this weird thing with running backs right now," Barkley said June 28. "Is it a difficult position to play? Yes. Do you take wear and tear? Yes. But who are you or anyone else to tell me how long I can play the game? I call [nonsense]."

"Some of the greats that I admire and I look up and study, they played well into their 30s. Barry [Sanders] left at 29, 30, and he left in his prime. It's what you put in. What you put in is what you get out. That's any position."

But what *does* Barkley put in?

Two thousand yards later and a few days removed from logging 31 carries against the Cowboys, he joked with a friend that his body didn't feel like it had just finished rushing for such a number. While Eagles coach Nick Sirianni elected to rest the majority of the team's starters in the regular-season finale against the Giants, Barkley said he would have been happy to invite another 20-plus carries in pursuit of Eric Dickerson's single-season rushing record if given the choice.

Part of the routine Barkley kept to stay fresh this season was plain to see. He typically goes through a circuit of light exercises at the start of Wednesday practices with Eagles senior athletic trainer Jerome Reid and often was listed as a limited participant during padded practices with a rest designation during the regular season.

Behind the scenes, Barkley's teammates suspect he's second only to right tackle Lane Johnson in money and time spent on recovery and rehabilitation during the season. Some estimated that his investment stretches into the six-figure mark annually, while others went so far as estimating he's around the $200,000 mark for measures that include massages, cold tubs, equipment, and physical therapy specialists to hasten his recovery process each week.

"He's got *people*," Eagles left tackle Jordan Mailata said.

While Barkley didn't have a specific number on what his annual expenditure is, he conceded that his teammates probably are on the lower side.

"Definitely over," he said. "But I've had way higher in the past."

"I don't know the exact number; I'd have to call my financial adviser. But I've put a lot of money into it, whether it's the offseason, whether it's your training with trainers or physical therapists. That's why I'm able to be the player I am right now. A couple high ankle sprains and a blown-out knee, to still be able to run at a high level and rush for 2,000 yards, it's not by mistake. I believe in the quote that 'Success is not an accident, it's not only the work you put into training but the work you put into taking care of yourself.'"

Defying the declining role of running backs in the modern NFL, Saquon Barkley led the league with 2,005 rushing yards, 345 carries, and 378 total touches during the regular season. (David Maialetti / Staff Photographer)

'Dark times'

There's a two-word refrain Gibson uses whenever he needs something more from Barkley during a training session.

"Dark times."

Based in the Washington area, Gibson typically travels to Barkley, first in Northern Jersey during his time with the Giants and closer to his native Whitehall last summer, and stay for three days to put Barkley through two daily workouts with a lifting session in between.

During that time, the former Villanova running back and Barkley will dive into the exacting nature of evading defenders.

The son of a boxer and the great-nephew of a former WBC middleweight champion, Barkley has a relationship with Gibson that can be likened to that of a boxer and a ringside coach. They pore over the action and the reaction that comes with every step or feint between a ballcarrier and a defender, closely mirroring the "sweet science" between the ropes.

Barkley, who even integrated boxing into his offseason regimen with his brother and uncle, said the parallels between the work he and Gibson do on the field and the work a fighter would do with his trainer isn't a coincidence.

"There's a reason why it's like that," Barkley said. "It comes from just the relationship that we've had since I was in college. He's been with me through it all. … He's been with me with my ACL, during the down years, the dark times."

Those "dark times," from the torn right ACL Barkley weathered early in his career to an unceremonious exit from the Giants after multiple offseasons of stagnant contract negotiations, are why Gibson coined the phrase and repeats it during training sessions.

He'll use the phrase on Barkley's social media posts or text it to him at random points during the season as well.

"It's like, 'You got here through hard work,'" Gibson said. "'Throughout some of the years because of your injuries, people have talked bad or people have put this dark cloud over you like you're a bad football player. It's a reminder to him that everybody does not root for you, and that's OK because everybody didn't root for you in the beginning.'

"I train boxers as well, and there's definitely a mentality he has. You keep swinging. You may fall, but you keep getting up and keep swinging. Because most people, when they do fall, when they feel the pressure or they're reading the comments from social media or whatever it may be, some people fall into it. 'Sa' is one of those people who continues to stand up, continues to fight, and continues to swing."

The messaging was a constant for Gibson this offseason. They typically met early in the morning at varying locations, wherever they could find grass. They'd break for a 90-minute lifting session afterward, followed by lunch. Then, often as the sun went down, they'd get back out on the grass for another two-plus hours going through drills to iron out the details of evading defenders, with a camera recording the entire session.

During one session, the slightest undulation in the turf led to Barkley obsessing over the footwork of one of Gibson's drills to the point where the trainer had to implore him to move on. He needed to reach the cone in three steps, but it was taking him four.

"I know I can be very detailed about training," Gibson said. "Like foot placement, stuff like that.

Saquon Barkley's breakout season with the Eagles followed "dark times" from his tenure with the New York Giants, which now serve as motivation. (Monica Herndon / Staff Photographer)

And I remember one time, he couldn't get this one drill down, and it killed him. It killed him to the point that we stayed on the drill longer than I wanted to be on the drill."

Barkley added: "The little details and stuff that we talk about on the thing, I love it. A lot of times, we'll be filming stuff so we'll have it on film where we're talking about little details on a run or on a cut and how it applies to the game. And then, boom, you turn on the film Sunday in October, and everything we talked about is happening within that run."

Watching Barkley's season mostly from afar, Gibson said, moments like that were the ones he remembered most.

"When he came in, he had a chip on his shoulder," Gibson said. "He didn't talk about it, but I could tell he did."

Pelletier, another trainer with whom Barkley often works during the offseason, noticed it as well. He'd use his connections to a local high school football program to get the school's field floodlights turned on so they could start before dawn.

They also go back about a decade. Pelletier played at Lehigh while Barkley was graduating high school. Pelletier said the level of detail Barkley brings to each drill stands out.

"I think what separates a lot of guys, and this goes for a lot of the pros I work with, is that they've already got God-gifted talents that are above most people," said Pelletier, who also trains Eagles wide receiver Jahan Dotson. "But their attention to detail is on another level. He's really locked into the details at all times, and for someone as gifted and talented as him, his attention to detail? That's what's going to make him one of the best ever."

2K over

As the Eagles reconvened for the first walk-through of the week on Wednesday, Barkley caught his teammates by surprise in the huddle.

"He's like, 'That 2,000 [stuff] is over. It's ... playoff time,'" Mailata said. "They're about to find out. I was like, 'Sir yes sir. Let's ... get it.'"

The regular season and its accolades now behind him, Barkley's next act begins against the Packers. It's just his second trip to the postseason; the first ended in a divisional-round loss to the Eagles in 2022 at Lincoln Financial Field.

After studying athletes like Michael Jordan and Kobe Bryant, Barkley isn't afraid to feed into narratives. If anyone doubts his ability to translate his regular-season success to the postseason, he'll be sure to use those doubts, drawing on the evenings spent under the lights with Gibson over the summer.

"We're still in dark times. Dark times don't change," Barkley said. "Sometimes the smile allows people to have a different opinion or view me different, but I'm always in that mode. No matter how much is said, especially this year, whether it's 2K or All-Pro or whatever, we're still in that 'dark times' mentality. It's me, [Gibson], and we're out there, and nobody is going to spare me reps and he's on my ass." ∎

While Saquon Barkley's regular season was defined by the march toward 2,000 rushing yards, his broader ambitions could only be accomplished in the playoffs. (Monica Herndon / Staff Photographer)

PLAYOFFS

JAN. 12, 2025
LINCOLN FINANCIAL FIELD
EAGLES 22, PACKERS 10

Moment of Brilliance

Zack Baun and the Eagles defense save the day as Jalen Hurts struggles in return

By Mike Sielski | Jan. 11, 2025

Only Jordan Love knows for certain what he saw when he dropped back on first down late in the second quarter, with the Green Bay Packers down 10 points but already inside Eagles territory and still on the move. There was no receiver in the middle of the field who was open, but Love threw the ball to the middle of the field anyway. The only player in position to catch the pass was linebacker Zack Baun, which was surprising only if you haven't been watching Baun play linebacker for the Eagles this season.

Baun intercepted Love's inexplicable pass, returning it 15 yards, snuffing out a Green Bay scoring threat — the most important play by a defense that was the NFL's best and needed to be at its best Sunday for the Eagles to win, 22-10.

"That was one of the best plays I've seen in a long time by a linebacker," said Eagles cornerback Darius Slay, who was in coverage behind Baun on the play. "He was throwing at my dude. It was going to be a bang-bang play, so I'd try to break it up. But to see him come into the picture like 'Pew-pew,' I said, 'Oooooooh.'

"The vision of him, just playing off of his guy because he had a dude in front of him. Just being a ballplayer, you know what I'm saying? 'Cause a guy could have said, 'Naw, I'm just looking at my guy and guarding my guy.' But he was actually like, 'I'm guarding my guy. Let me see what the quarterback's doing.' And he came off his dude and made a play. That's big-time, man. Not a lot of linebackers can do that."

Baun's moment of brilliance stood out in a game that otherwise was as enjoyable as having someone close a door on your fingers: too many penalties, too many mistakes, a couple of quarterbacks, in Love and Jalen Hurts, who missed too many throws and made too many poor decisions. The Eagles' saving grace, as it has been since mid-October, was their defense. The unit that gave up the fewest yards and second-fewest points in the league during the regular season showed just one weakness against the Packers: a relative inability to tackle running back Josh Jacobs. And given that the 5-foot-10, 223-pound Jacobs had rushed for 1,329 yards and 15 touchdowns this season, there was only so much

Linebacker Zack Baun runs past the Green Bay Packers bench after an interception late in the second quarter of the wild-card playoff game. (Yong Kim / Staff Photographer)

shame in that flaw. The Eagles forced four turnovers, intercepted Love three times, sacked him twice, and held the Packers to their lowest point total of the season, and Baun was at the center of it all, with seven tackles and his timely pick.

"By no means was it a clean game by any of us," he said, "but to hold a team like that to 10 points gives us confidence."

He had begun his remarkable season with a remarkable game in São Paulo, Brazil, against the Packers: 15 tackles, two sacks of Love, two hits on Love. After four years as mostly a special-teamer with the New Orleans Saints, after signing a one-year, $3.5 million contract with the Eagles in the offseason, after never having played inside linebacker until defensive coordinator Vic Fangio trusted his eyes and experience and moved him there in training camp, Baun is the consummate representation of the Eagles' success. Fangio and player-personnel chief Howie Roseman collaborated to create an All-Pro inside linebacker pretty much out of thin air, and it should lead to a financial windfall for Baun in free agency.

"Yeahhh, man," Slay said. "I hope it's us, but somebody going to pay that man big bucks."

First things first: Baun will likely have to raise his level of play next week in the divisional round. Nakobe Dean left Sunday's game with a knee injury and was on crutches when he exited the locker room afterward. Oren Burks has filled in capably before, and while the burden on Baun will be greater for Dean's absence, he has given no indication that he can't handle it.

"What you see with Zack is just a guy that's tough, physical, loves football, great work ethic," Eagles head coach Nick Sirianni had said Friday.

"Those guys [who] have all that usually have an opportunity to reach their ceiling, and he just keeps getting better. So I don't think we know what his ceiling is. You know, he keeps getting better with every rep that he gets on the inside at linebacker — very versatile, the different things that he can do. He's worked really hard at that."

It's difficult to find a game this season when Baun and his teammates had to work harder than Sunday's. The Eagles offense was that sluggish. Whether he was still feeling the effects of his Dec. 22 concussion or not, Hurts was spotty at best; after completing his first six passes, he struggled against the Packers' pass rush and fell back into the hesitancy that caused so much consternation for his receivers a few weeks ago.

The only reason to think that the Eagles can reach the Super Bowl with Hurts playing like he did Sunday is their defense, and had Baun not snared that Love pass just before halftime, had the Packers scored there to cut the Eagles' lead to three before the break, who knows what might have happened in the second half? No Zack Baun on Sunday, no Zack Baun this season, and how different would everything be for the Eagles? "You don't put any limits on players," Fangio said. "If you put limits on them, you'll get limited production. Take them to the ceiling that they can go to." He's playing like he hasn't reached his yet. It's as good a reason as any to think the Eagles can still reach theirs. ∎

Eagles cornerbacks Avonte Maddox and Quinyon Mitchell prevent Packers wide receiver Romeo Doubs from making a touchdown catch. (David Maialetti / Staff Photographer)

NFC DIVISIONAL PLAYOFF

JAN. 19, 2025
LINCOLN FINANCIAL FIELD
EAGLES 28, RAMS 22

No Limits

Jalen Carter preserves the Eagles' Super Bowl hopes

By Mike Sielski

Within the dry and cozy comfort of the Eagles' locker room Sunday, Jalen Carter was describing how he saved their season. A little stunt in the team's defensive playbook, Carter faking an inside move then swinging his right arm over Los Angeles Rams center Beaux Limmer, had sent him surging straight at quarterback Matthew Stafford for a sack.

One play later, one more Carter hit on Stafford for good measure, the Eagles were celebrating a 28-22 divisional-round victory and a trip to the NFC championship game, and now Carter made that whole closing sequence sound like the most natural thing in the world.

"That's all it was," he said. "I ran the stunt, and they messed up their communication on the O-line."

To Carter's right, his teammate Moro Ojomo returned to his locker after taking a shower.

"This," he said, nodding at Carter, "is the best defensive tackle in the country."

Talent to spare

Back in early September, when the only snow to be found came in a paper cone courtesy of Mister Softee, Carter spent several minutes one afternoon talking about the "rookie wall" that he insisted he hadn't hit in 2023. He had been a rookie-of-the-year candidate for the first half of last season, so dominant at defensive tackle that it was obvious that the Eagles' dare to take him with the ninth pick in the draft had paid off for them. Then the Eagles, in every aspect, fell apart over the season's final seven weeks, and Carter's production slowed and the quality of his play declined, and months later, it was fair to ask why and whether he was past it.

"No, I don't feel like I hit a wall," he said then. "There's a lot of excuses people are saying about what happened last year. I ain't got no excuses. What happened, happened. We're on to this year."

This year for the Eagles already is better, already has surpassed the low standard of that horrid late-season slump of '23, and Carter is both a reason and a symbol for the team's resurgence. The Eagles are one victory away from their third Super Bowl appearance in eight years, and from Carter to Saquon Barkley, from Zack Baun to Dallas Goedert, they have accumulated so much talent that they're not only strong enough to beat a formidable opponent — and

Eagles defensive tackle Jalen Carter goes after Rams running back Kyren Williams. (Yong Kim / Staff Photographer)

the Rams were one — but also capable of overcoming their own weaknesses and errors.

The roster that Howie Roseman and his staff have put together sometimes allows the Eagles to win in spite of themselves.

Which is exactly what they did Sunday. They showed their few weaknesses and made plenty of mistakes, and the everlasting irony of this season is that, as great as the Eagles have been at times, the area that they considered for years to be essential to their success — to the success of any team that sought to be among the NFL's elite — has been their softest target. Their passing game was a problem against the Rams, Jalen Hurts holding the ball too long too often, managing just 128 yards through the air, taking a safety that pulled Los Angeles within a point late in the third quarter that made every frozen fan at The Linc nervous as hell.

But on the Rams' next possession, Carter kicked off a stretch of play that demonstrated why Ojomo might be right, why Carter should be considered not just the best player on the Eagles' defense but one of the best defensive players in the entire league. He punched the football out of the hands of Rams running back Kyren Williams, forcing a fumble that cornerback Isaiah Rodgers recovered and returned 40 yards to set up a Jake Elliott field goal.

"We work on that every week," Carter said. "Punch it out. Got one last time we played them in L.A. I knew it was a possibility we could get it again. It was on my mind. The opportunity came."

That fumble, in and of itself, was a game-turner, but it was only a prelude to the two most important defensive plays any Eagle has made all season. Stafford had the Rams moving, and somehow back in the game after a 78-yard Barkley TD run had seemingly buried them.

And on third-and-2 from the Eagles' 13-yard line,

with less than 80 seconds standing between the Eagles and one of the most stunning and excruciating losses in the city's sports history, Carter burst through the line like a bull and sacked Stafford. A 9-yard loss. Fourth down now, and this time Carter charged through again, forcing Stafford into a quick throw that sailed out of bounds, driving him to the ground. Watch a replay of those two moments. No 6-foot-3, 314-pound man should be able to move that fast.

"He was born to play football: prototypical size, frame, strength, athleticism, speed," Eagles defensive tackle Milton Williams said. "He's everything you want in a D-lineman."

Two sacks, two tackles for losses, three quarterback hits — Carter provided every ounce of validation that the Eagles could have asked for when they took the chance on drafting him last year. He'd been a marvelous player but an immature kid at the University of Georgia, had been involved in a tragic road-racing accident that led to the deaths of two people, and there was plenty of risk in the Eagles' decision to bet on him.

By all indications, though, he has caused no trouble here, at least nothing major. The one hiccup happened in November '23, a rumor on social media that Carter had stolen items from a Target store, an incident that police investigated and determined was no crime.

"We're always going off what he say-she say," Carter said after Sunday's game. "You ask anybody in this locker room. I feel like everybody loves me. I've got a good connection with everybody in this locker room. We're all having fun, and we've all got one goal. In college, it was getting a natty. In the pros, it's getting a Super Bowl.

"I'm matured, of course. You see what's going on in the locker room, everything. You see what's on the field. But I'm still me. I'm still chill. In college,

Saquon Barkley runs for a 78-yard touchdown in the fourth quarter as the snow falls at Lincoln Financial Field. (David Maialetti / Staff Photographer)

I stayed home, played games all day. I'm doing the same thing. Obviously, when I get a family, I'll move around, do this, do that, but right now, I'm chilling, just young, 23 years old, playing football, trying to get a Super Bowl for the guys."

Two wins away after Sunday, after Carter showed everyone that he was becoming — if he hasn't already become — the player the Eagles thought and hoped he would be.

"It's still a team sport," he said. "Just like when I play and need them, when they play, they need me."

Never more than in those final seconds against Stafford and the Rams, with a shot at the Super Bowl on the line. Never more than in a snowy setting that no one will forget. Nope, no wall for Jalen Carter. No limits. No excuses. Just a great game when the Eagles had to have one. ■

JAN. 26, 2025
LINCOLN FINANCIAL FIELD
EAGLES 55, COMMANDERS 23

Eyes on the Prize

Saquon Barkley's three touchdowns lead Eagles to Super Bowl

By Jeff Neiburg

The party was on at Lincoln Financial Field. The confetti was falling, and the stage was set. But Saquon Barkley was heading through the southwest tunnel of the stadium as Eagles fans serenaded him with "MVP" chants.

After six seasons of mostly losing with the New York Giants, Barkley wanted to find his family. But he was going the wrong way, and so the Eagles' MVP candidate, the one who broke and chased records throughout the regular season and these playoffs, made a U-turn and went back to the field to find them.

Jeffrey Lurie held a trophy high. Jalen Hurts and A.J. Brown were on the stage. But Barkley never went to the stage. He did a few interviews on the field, but then it was time to find his loved ones. And when the Eagles finally made their way toward their locker room, there was Saquon Jr. in his father's hands, and the rest of the Barkley clan flanking the player most responsible for the Eagles reaching the Super Bowl.

"It was fun to be out there and see the confetti and things you envision, but the most special thing about it was being out there with my family," Barkley said. "I know I've never been there, but I've been there so many times in my head."

This, the celebration, the shot at a Super Bowl, was why Barkley signed with the Eagles, he said.

"That's one of the first conversations I had with Howie [Roseman]," Barkley said. "That's the conversation I had with my family. I came to Philly to be a part of games like this, and none better than a game when you can advance to the Super Bowl."

He started it with a bang.

Barkley has spent the duration of the season being an opposing defense's worst nightmare. Sunday afternoon, he was his own, if only for a brief moment.

The Eagles defense was on the field for 18 plays on a grueling opening drive from Washington that featured a pair of third-and-6 conversions and another two conversions on fourth down. The Eagles defense held the Commanders to three points and needed a rest, but Barkley had other ideas.

The defense rested for one play.

Will Shipley gave the Eagles good field position with a 35-yard return to the Eagles' 40-yard line, and Jalen Hurts led the offense onto

Saquon Barkley avoids defensive end Clelin Ferrell during the fourth quarter of the NFC championship game against the Washington Commanders. (Yong Kim / Staff Photographer)

the field. Hurts checked into a new play. It sent DeVonta Smith in motion as Hurts took an under-center snap from Landon Dickerson, who started in place of Cam Jurgens. It was a fake jet sweep and a pitch to Barkley.

Out to the left side, Jordan Mailata and Dallas Goedert made a hole. Barkley took care of the rest. He broke through safety Quan Martin's arm tackle, then safety Jeremy Chinn had two chances to bring Barkley down and couldn't. Barkley cut to his right at Washington's 35-yard line and was gone.

Eagles 7, Commanders 3, and the Eagles never trailed again in their 55-23 NFC championship victory.

"We wanted to send a message and we did that," Barkley said. "We knew that when you play a team two or three times, they kind of get a bead on some of your stuff. We gave them a dummy call and it worked to perfection."

It was the first of three touchdowns for Barkley, and his record-setting season will have one more stop: New Orleans.

The Eagles won all three of their home playoff games in different ways, but Barkley, as he has been all season, was the constant. He racked up 119 rushing yards in a wild-card win over the Green Bay Packers, added 205 and two scores last week vs. the Los Angeles Rams, and finished Sunday with 118.

His 4-yard touchdown extended the Eagles' lead to 14-3 late in the first quarter, and he bookended his opening-play score with another 4-yard touchdown midway through the fourth quarter. On that last touchdown, Hurts took a shotgun snap from Jurgens, who came into the game in the second half after Dickerson went down with a knee injury. Hurts handed to Barkley, who cut right and waltzed into the end zone as the Eagles blocked the play perfectly.

Barkley put his hands together and placed them under his chin as he ran around the back of the end zone miming a "good night" message to the Commanders.

John Mara's restless nights will continue. The Giants' owner said he would lose sleep if Barkley went to the Eagles, but who could have seen all of this?

Maybe Tonya Johnson, Saquon's mother.

"You ever been on a job sometimes and it doesn't work out and then you get in a new job and you flourish?" she said. "That's how things work sometimes. That's how the universe is.

"It's been great for him to finally be somewhere where he's able to showcase his talent without people talking about him, without this, without that, running backs don't deserve this, they don't deserve that. Now we see.

"I'm excited. It's been a long time coming. It's been a dream of his since he was a kid. And we're going to win, by the way."

Barkley wasn't making any similar proclamations in the locker room, but he did mention that there was still unfinished business.

"We've done a lot of special stuff," Barkley said. "But the most special thing you can do is win a Super Bowl. That's our goal. Obviously I wasn't here two years ago, but I bought into this culture, I bought into this organization, and I know how those guys felt. I'm going to make sure I do everything in my capability to make sure the same thing won't happen again."

With the offense humming like it was Sunday, and the Eagles defense being a turnover-forcing machine, a different result is in sight.

The Eagles rushed for seven touchdowns. Hurts added three of his own, two of which came via the Tush Push. Shipley later scored a garbage-time touchdown after Nick Sirianni gave Hurts a curtain call with a timeout and inserted Kenny Pickett at quarterback. By the time Shipley scored, 3 minutes, 3 seconds remained on the clock and the party was more than on throughout the Delaware Valley.

Hurts had his best game since returning from a concussion he suffered during a Week 16 loss at Washington. He was efficient and took care of the

Wide receivers A.J. Brown and DeVonta Smith douse Nick Sirianni with Gatorade as the Eagles secured the NFC championship. (David Maialetti / Staff Photographer)

football and made good use of A.J. Brown, Smith, and Goedert.

But everything is always easier with the threat of Barkley.

"It's a good day," Tonya said. "It's the 26th. His number is 26. His birthday is February the 9th, the Super Bowl is February the 9th."

Barkley didn't get a chance to best Eric Dickerson's single-season rushing record as the Eagles rested their starters in their meaningless regular-season finale. But he'll have a chance at the Super Bowl in two weeks to set a record for the most rushing yards in a season when combining the regular season and postseason. He entered Sunday 148 yards shy of Terrell Davis' record-setting 1998 season when he compiled 2,476 yards.

He'll need another 30 in New Orleans.

Don't blink, it might take only one play. ■

'He's a Winner'

Jalen Hurts quiets haters in NFC championship victory

By Marcus Hayes | Jan. 26, 2025

"All he does is win!"

That was Nick Sirianni's message to the world after Jalen Hurts carried Sirianni back to the Super Bowl.

Moments later, a classic from DJ Khaled blasted from the speakers at Lincoln Financial Field: "All I do is win, win, win, no matter what!"

Hurts did more than just win Sunday evening. He blew up. He cemented his worth. He comforted anyone who still questions a $255 million contract for a 195-yard passer in a league that has devolved into flag football with shoulder pads.

Hurts and his offense scored 55 points Sunday, the most in any conference championship game and the second-highest total in the club's 54 playoff games. Hurts went 20-for-28 for 246 yards, with a passing touchdown, a running touchdown, and two Tush Push scores. He found A.J. Brown on fourth-and-5 for 31 yards down the sideline to set up a touchdown late in the second quarter. He left the game with 3 minutes, 53 seconds to play to a wild ovation, his last game at the Linc until September, but not his last game of the year.

Hurts and his Eagles have next week off before heading to New Orleans for Super Bowl LIX on Feb. 9. They will face the Kansas City Chiefs, who edged the Buffalo Bills in the AFC championship game on Sunday night.

It's only the fifth time in 17 games he's started and finished this season that Hurts threw for at least 240 yards, and he indicated that the game plans devised by coordinator Kellen Moore and Sirianni have kept Hurts conservative by design.

"I guess he let me out of my straitjacket a little bit today," Hurts said with a grin.

Make no mistake: Hurts, who usually is a retiring sort, was feeling himself Sunday night. After the game, a tan suit coat draped over his arm, wearing a black, collarless shirt, with a black-and-silver NFC champions hat on backward, he strolled into the coaches' offices to pose with the George Halas Trophy. Hurts put his arm around owner Jeffrey Lurie on his right and GM Howie Roseman on his left, a fat cigar in his teeth, and waited for the photo flash. A few minutes later, back at his locker, he lit it.

He'd earned it.

The Eagles' road to the Super Bowl was paved by Saquon Barkley's unmatched season as a runner and the best Eagles defense since the Minister himself, Reggie White, added to his legend 35 years ago. Sirianni's humility as a head coach, Moore's innovation as a coordinator, and Vic Fangio's defensive genius created a culture of comfortable competence and maximal execution. The Eagles forced four turnovers in their 55-23 win over the

After an uneven regular season and a recent concussion, Jalen Hurts rose to the occasion in the NFC championship game, going 20-for-28 for 246 yards. (Yong Kim / Staff Photographer)

visiting Washington Commanders on Sunday evening. Barkley ran for 118 yards and scored three touchdowns on 15 carries.

But without Hurts, it's all for nothing.

Without Hurts, Sirianni doesn't get to go to two Super Bowls in three years.

"He deals with so much criticism, which just blows my mind," Sirianni said. "Man, this guy wins. Winning, at quarterback, is more important than any stat that you go through."

Hurts agreed.

"It's not about me. I don't even play the game for any statistical measure. Nothing more than just winning," Hurts said. "You play the game to win."

His teammates love that attitude.

"I feel great for him," Barkley said. "I'm not taking anything away from Jalen, but — he's Jalen Hurts, man! He wins. He doesn't get his respect. But if we win this next game, they're going to have to give it to him."

As for the argument that Hurts succeeds because of Barkley and A.J. Brown and a great offensive line, Sirianni noted that great QBs seldom thrive on their own: Joe Montana had Jerry Rice and great backs, Tom Brady had Rob Gronkowski and Randy Moss, Patrick Mahomes had Tyreek Hill and Travis Kelce.

"You tell me a quarterback who's won like this that has [crap players] around him," Sirianni said.

It is a great team, though, the best in Eagles history. It also has its best GM, Roseman, and its best owner, Lurie. None of that would matter without Jalen Hurts.

Lurie might have kept Howie and Nick on board when their critics were calling for their heads, and he might have pushed to draft Hurts and pushed to pay Hurts the most money in franchise history. Roseman might have shopped for the groceries. The coaches might have concocted this potent stew.

All of that paved the road.

Jalen Hurts drove the bus.

Hurts entered the game injured, having twisted his knee against the Los Angeles Rams the week before. He'd missed the final two games of the regular season with a concussion. He also was sick Sunday night.

Hurts entered the game embattled, having finished the season averaging just over 193 passing yards per game, then averaging less than 130 yards in the two playoff wins that sent him to the NFC championship game.

He exited the game a winner. Again.

He was 39-4 in college. He's 51-23 as a pro. If he gets No. 52, he'll become the greatest QB in franchise history. Low bar, maybe, but it is what it is.

He speaks in aphorisms and parables, and he often refers to "The Standard." What is his standard, he was asked Sunday.

"The standard is to win," he replied.

In an era defined by analytics and statistics, how did he become so obsessed with winning?

"By losing."

Sirianni loves that.

"I don't want anybody else leading this team at quarterback other than him," Sirianni said. "He's a winner."

Hurts has been dissected and minimized, often evaluated for what he's not instead of for what he is.

Embattled and questioned and criticized for much of the last two seasons for everything from aptitude to attitude, Hurts has reached the Super Bowl for the second time in just four seasons as a starter. Most of the critics — from the stat-rich, win-poor legends to the talking-head failed NFL backups — cannot say the same. Most of them weren't winners. Not winners like Jalen Hurts.

Hurts isn't the NFL's best quarterback. He can't throw it like Josh Allen and Joe Burrow, never could, never will. He can't run like Commanders rookie Jayden Daniels or Ravens superman Lamar Jackson; at least, he can't anymore. He doesn't

The Eagles are crowned NFC champions after a decisive 55-23 win over the Washington Commanders. (Yong Kim / Staff Photographer)

diagnose defenses like Matthew Stafford, and he doesn't have the magic of Mahomes.

You know what he does? He wins. And wins. And wins.

Hurts makes the plays that need to be made, with his legs, or his arm, or his brain, and Hurts protects the football like a momma bear protects her cubs. He has committed just three turnovers since Game 4. The Eagles are 13-0 in the last 13 games he both started and finished. His passer rating in that stretch is 102.7, which would have ranked sixth in the regular season, just behind ...

Whattaya know? Jalen Hurts!

Yep, he's been this efficient all year long. Not especially pretty, and not especially productive, but pretty production doesn't always win unless it's efficient, and Hurts has been a model of efficiency.

So he isn't Favre or Montana or Brady or Rodgers.

He isn't supposed to be.

What he is, is, a stone-cold winner.

With one more win to go. ■